# Ripley's Believe It or Not!

**19th Series**

D1547983

PUBLISHED BY POCKET BOOKS NEW YORK

**RIPLEY'S BELIEVE IT OR NOT!® 19TH SERIES**

POCKET BOOK edition published December, 1972

 ─────────────────────

This original POCKET BOOK edition is printed from brand-new plates.
POCKET BOOK editions are published by POCKET BOOKS, a division of
Simon & Schuster, Inc., 630 Fifth Avenue, New York, N.Y. 10020.
Trademarks registered in the United States and other countries.
                                                                    L

# PREFACE

Martin Klaver of Hamburg, Germany, was a complete man of the nineteenth century. He was born on January 1, 1801, and died December 31, 1900. Thus, he did not miss a single day of the entire century. We should not make the mistake of thinking that the calendar century began on January 1, 1800, and ended December 31, 1899.

A man named "Onze" (11) married a woman named "Huit" (8) in Lyon, France, in 1893. When their first son was born she named him "Dix-neuf" (19). The officiating priest objected that there was no such baptismal name in the entire Christian hagiology. She explained she had added the two surnames. She had her way.

A lady named Kane in Los Angeles, who bestowed the name "Hurry" on her first born, replied to our inquiry that she had chosen this name after seeing it in a *Believe It or Not!* cartoon in which we told of a previous occasion when the offspring of a Kane family was named "Hurry."

Guillermo Despacio of Uruguay married twice. He had 19 daughters by his first wife, and 19 sons by his second. And where did it happen—in a town named "19 of April."

If we dwelt on the number 19 in this Preface, it was our aim to demonstrate the inexhaustible resources of our *Believe It or Not!* archives. In placing the *Ripley's Believe It or Not! 19th Series* in your hands, we proudly stress the innumerable and choice cartoons it contains. No effort was spared to make this new edition a front-runner in fascination. We know of no other collection so bound to cater to, and to whet, human curiosity.

And finally we'd like to bestow an accolade on our distinguished Art Director, Paul Frehm.

—Norbert Pearlroth
Research Director
BELIEVE IT OR NOT!

## THE STREET PAVED WITH MOTHER-OF-PEARL

THE MAIN THOROUGHFARE OF DENHAM, IN WESTERN AUSTRALIA, IS COVERED WITH THE SHELLS OF THE PEARL OYSTER-- *ITS IRIDESCENT COLORS PROVIDING AN EVER-CHANGING PATTERN*

**TRIPLET CALVES BORN TO A HOLSTEIN COW**

## GIOVAMBATISTA STROZZI

(1488-1538) of FLORENCE, ITALY, AFTER STABBING HIMSELF TO AVOID IMPRISONMENT, AS HIS LAST DYING ACT WROTE WITH THE BLOODY TIP OF HIS SWORD: **"MAY MY AVENGER ARISE OUT OF MY BONES"**

## DOM VITAL ZUCCOLO

(1556-1630) A SCHOLARLY PRIEST OF PADUA, ITALY, *WAS NEVER SEEN WITHOUT A BOOK OR PEN IN HIS HAND*

## A COIN SHORTAGE

IN BIRMINGHAM, ENGLAND, IN 1773, LED THE BIRMINGHAM BANK TO ISSUE *ROUND, 7-SHILLING PAPER COINS*

7

**MOUNTAIN MUSIC**
Hohenseelbach, Germany
A MOUNTAIN CONSISTING OF HEXAGONAL STONE COLUMNS **70** FEET HIGH WHICH ACT LIKE THE STRINGS OF A GIGANTIC AEOLIAN HARP --*PRODUCING A MELODY WHENEVER THE WIND STRUMS THEM*

**King PERSEUS**
WHO RULED MACEDONIA FROM 178 TO 168 B.C. WAS EXECUTED BY HIS ROMAN CAPTORS *BY KEEPING HIM AWAKE UNTIL HE DIED OF EXHAUSTION*

A **MARRIAGE RECORD** REQUESTED FROM THE CLERK OF BOURBON COUNTY, KENTUCKY, ON THE WEDDING OF ISAAC ORCHARD AND MARGERA MITCHELL, WAS DECLARED IMPOSSIBLE TO LOCATE *BECAUSE SUCH RECORDS WERE ALL BALED--AND THE ORCHARD MARRIAGE HAD TAKEN PLACE 159 YEARS BEFORE*

AT THAT, BETTY JO DENTON HEICK, THE COUNTY CLERK, POKED ONE OF THE DUSTY BALES ON A HIGH SHELF, AND DOWN FLOATED A SINGLE PIECE OF PAPER--*THE MARRIAGE BOND OF ISAAC ORCHARD AND MARGERA MITCHELL, DATED SEPTEMBER 29, 1791*

**A TRANSISTOR RADIO** POWERED BY A SMALL BATTERY WAS FOUND BY MARK BARASH'S DOG IN BUSHES IN *WHICH IT HAD BEEN LOST 4 YEARS BEFORE --AND IT STILL PLAYED PERFECTLY*
Old Bethpage, L.I., N.Y.

**FRANÇOIS VIÈTE**
( 1540-1603 )
A FRENCHMAN WHO WAS THE LEADING MATHEMATICIAN OF HIS TIME, COULD NOT SLEEP EXCEPT ON A PILLOW BENEATH WHICH HE HAD STASHED *HIS ENTIRE FORTUNE OF $20,000 -- IN CASH*

**THE UNEASY HEAD**
BALANCING BOULDER *SHAPED LIKE A HUMAN HEAD* NEAR THE WESTERN BORDER OF COLORADO

**PATRICK HALLINAN** OF SAN FRANCISCO, CALIF., AND 3 OF HIS BROTHERS *ALL WON INTRA-MURAL BOXING CHAMP-IONSHIPS AT THE UNIV. OF CALIF.*

**LATVIAN POSTAGE STAMPS** IN 1920 WERE PRINTED ON THE BLANK BACKS OF CURRENCY ISSUED IN WORLD WAR I TO GERMAN SOLDIERS

9

## DOWN HALL

AN ESTATE IN ENGLAND, WAS BOUGHT BY POET MATTHEW PRIOR IN 1719 FOR $20,370 -- *THE SUM PAID HIM FOR WRITING A BOOK OF POETRY*

## FERNANDO d'AVALOS

(1490-1525) LATER COMMANDER OF THE SPANISH ARMY, WAS CAPTURED IN THE BATTLE OF RAVENNA BY THE FRENCH WHEN HE WAS 16 YEARS OF AGE, AND EVEN THEN WAS CONSIDERED SO IMPORTANT AN OFFICER THAT HIS RANSOM WAS FIXED AT 6,000 PIECES OF SILVER -- *ONE COIN FOR EACH DAY OF HIS LIFE*

A **MONUMENT TO A HEN**
A PLAQUE IN ADAMSVILLE, RHODE IS., *WHERE THE RHODE ISLAND HEN ORIGINATED*

## THE PUBLIC FOUNTAIN

IN LIMOGES, FRANCE, IS MADE OF *THE FINEST LIMOGES CHINA*

**2 GLASSES**
FOUND SEALED IN A WALL IN BRESLAU, GERMANY, IN 1936 *STILL WERE FILLED WITH BEER AFTER 210 YEARS*

THE **CHAIR** IN WHICH PRINCESS ADÉLAÏDE, SISTER OF KING LOUIS PHILIPPE OF FRANCE, DIED ON DEC. 31, 1847, STILL STANDS IN THE CASTLE OF RANDAN, FRANCE, WITH HER ROBE AND FOOTSTOOL--*UNDISTURBED FOR 122 YEARS*

**MARY BEAN**
1726-1826 of Lynn, Mass.,
COULD THREAD A NEEDLE SWIFTLY WITHOUT THE AID OF EYEGLASSES -*AT THE AGE OF 100*

A **HUGE CONCRETE PILLAR** MARKS A BORDER POINT *WHERE SWEDEN, NORWAY AND FINLAND MEET*

THE **OLD GONZAGA COLLEGE**, IN SPOKANE, WASH., A SOLID-BRICK STRUCTURE WEIGHING 2,500,000 LBS., *WAS TURNED 45 DEGREES IN 1900 AND MOVED 175 FEET WITHOUT BREAKING A SINGLE BRICK*

**ANT INNS**
SOME ANTS IN CONSIDERATION FOR THEIR TIRED WORKERS, BUILD SHELTERS ALONG THE TRAILS THEY FOLLOW *SO THEY CAN REST DURING THEIR LABORS*

THE **BAGPIPER WHO PIPED HIS OWN LIFE AWAY!**

**DONALD DOBBIE** of Lauder, Scotland, PLAYED THE BAGPIPES FOR **12** HOURS, THEN CONTINUED TO PLAY THEM ON A WALK OF **7** MILES TO WIN A WAGER —

*BUT AS HE COLLECTED HIS BET HE DIED OF EXHAUSTION*

THE **MEMORIAL** TO MURDER
THE CASTLE OF BARBOTAN IN FRANCE WAS DEMOLISHED AS PART OF THE PUNISHMENT OF ITS OWNER, WHO KILLED JULIEN DE LORGERIL, IN 1649, *BUT ITS TOWER WAS LEFT STANDING TO COMMEMORATE THE SLAYING*

12

**THE WOOD LIBRARY**
OF CASTLE GUTTENBERG,
Germany,
CONSISTS OF **97** VOLUMES
*EACH BOUND IN A
DIFFERENT VARIETY
OF TREE BARK*

THE **MALE MIDWIFE FROG**
HE HATCHES THE EGGS
PRODUCED BY HIS MATE BY
CARRYING THEM AROUND
*AFFIXED TO HIS OWN BODY*

The **PEPPERBOX**
Brighton,
England,
BUILT OVER
A WELL IN
THE HEALTH
RESORT BY
KING GEORGE IV
*AS A TRIBUTE
TO PEPPER'S
CONTRIBUTION
TO BRITISH
WEALTH*

**W**OMEN of the Lapo Tribe,
of Yunnan, China,
WEAR MINI SKIRTS IF THEY ARE
POOR -- *AND MAXI SKIRTS
IF THEY ARE WEALTHY*

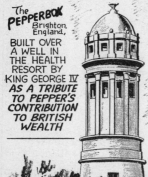

TURKHEN
A
CROSS
BETWEEN A
TURKEY
AND A
CHICKEN

13

HOLDEN, THE OLD ASTRONOMER DISCOVERED THAT THE EARTH WAS FLAT AND STATIONARY AND THAT THE SUN AND THE MOON DO MOVE

EPITAPH OF PROF. JOSEPH W. HOLDEN (1816-1900) in Elmwood Cemetery, East Otisfield, Me.

## LADY DELORAINE

(1700-1744)

GOVERNESS TO BRITAIN'S ROYAL PRINCESSES, PLAYFULLY PULLED AWAY A CHAIR AS KING GEORGE II WAS ABOUT TO SIT DOWN --*AND THE MONARCH SPRAWLED ON THE FLOOR IN FRONT OF HIS COURT* SHE WAS DISCHARGED AS A GOVERNESS, BUT NOT OTHERWISE PUNISHED

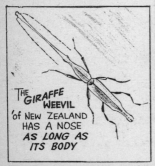

THE *GIRAFFE WEEVIL* of NEW ZEALAND HAS A NOSE *AS LONG AS ITS BODY*

**THE TOMB of ST. MENOUX** in St. Menoux Church, Moulins, France, HAS **3** OPENINGS THROUGH WHICH A PILGRIM CAN PUSH HIS HEAD *AS A CURE FOR HEADACHES*

THE **NEST** OF THE SUNBIRD, of Borneo, IS A CUP-SHAPED MASS OF VEGETABLE FIBERS WHICH THE BIRD LASHES TO THE UNDERSIDE OF A LEAF BY SEWING IT IN PLACE WITH THREADS STOLEN FROM A *SPIDER'S WEB*

THE **PEDESTAL ROCKS** Bad Wildstein, Germany 3 UPRIGHT ROCKS SUPPORTING A COLUMN OF STONES TOPPED BY A HUGE, FLAT BOULDER —*WITHOUT THE USE OF MORTAR*

**SARGASSO FISH** IN THE WEED-COVERED SARGASSO SEA, HAVE WEEDLIKE PROTUBERANCES, AND EVEN CHANGE THE COLOR AND DESIGN OF IMPRINTS ON THEIR BODIES THAT *RESEMBLE WEEDS*

**STALACTITE DRAPERIES** in the Caves of Cheddar, England *NATURAL FORMATION*

**CAPTAIN SLASH,** A DESPERADO IN Northampton, Eng., IRKED BECAUSE HIS NEIGHBORS HAD PROPHESIED HE WOULD DIE WITH HIS BOOTS ON *KICKED HIS SHOES INTO THE CROWD OF SPECTATORS AS HE WAS BEING HANGED* 1826

**THE OLDEST BREWERY IN THE WORLD**
THE BAVARIAN STATE BREWERY, IN WEIHENSTEPHAN, BAVARIA, *HAS BEEN BREWING BEER FOR 824 YEARS*

THE **NEST** of the YELLOW WEAVER BIRD of Java, SUSPENDED BETWEEN REEDS AND WEIGHED DOWN WITH STONES SO ITS EGGS WILL NOT FALL OUT -- *LETS THE WAVING REEDS SLIDE THROUGH IT AS IF IT WERE A PULLEY*

**ST. JOHN** A VILLAGE ON THE ISLAND OF CRETE, GREECE, COMPRISING WEDGE-SHAPED WINDOWLESS STONE HOUSES CARVED OUT OF A MOUNTAIN, *IS INVISIBLE TO ANYONE STANDING JUST ABOVE IT*

THE **CHIEF** of the BOAR SOCIETY of the DAN TRIBE of West Africa, TO PROVE THAT HE CAN EMULATE A WILD BOAR, MUST THROW *SAND IN HIS OWN EYES*

THE **RIALTO BRIDGE** in Venice,
ALTHOUGH BUILT ON 12,000 PILES DRIVEN INTO THE MARSHY GROUND,
*WAS CONSIDERED UNSAFE UNTIL 2 ROWS OF SOUVENIR
SHOPS WERE BUILT ON THE SPAN TO STABILIZE IT*

THE
**FLYING CUTTLEFISH**
(Stenoteuthis bartrami)
FLIES OUT OF THE WATER
*BY JET PROPULSION—*
IT DISCHARGES A JET
OF WATER WITH SUCH
FORCE THAT IT FLIES
A DISTANCE OF 35 FEET,
15 FEET IN THE AIR,
AT A SPEED OF
ABOUT *20* NAUTICAL
MILES AN HOUR

THE
**RED-CRESTED WOODPECKER**
TO ENABLE IT
TO HOOK GRUBS
FROM DECAYING
TREES, *HAS A
TONGUE BARBED
WITH SHARP
BRISTLES*

**ANTONIO JOSÉ HERRERA**
of Albuquerque, N.M.,
*GREW A COMPLETE
3d SET OF TEETH*
ALL OF HIS TEETH WERE
KICKED OUT BY A HORSE
WHEN HE WAS 10
YEARS OF AGE

17

**FIELD MARSHAL JAN von WERTH** (1594-1652) of Germany SMOKED A PIPE, CHEWED TOBACCO AND SNUFFED IT **SIMULTANEOUSLY**

A **TRUMPET** USED BY A SECRET SOCIETY IN TOGO, AFRICA, IS ENCRUSTED WITH HUMAN JAWBONES

MRS. **JANE GIDSCOMBE** of No. Creek, Ky., WAS SAVED FROM INJURY WHEN A CYCLONE DESTROYED HER HOME BECAUSE *A HEAVY LOOM FELL ON HER* — THE LOOM WHICH DROPPED FROM THE SECOND STORY OF THE HOUSE, SERVED AS A SHELTER WHEN BRICKS FROM THE CHIMNEY CRASHED DOWN WHERE MRS. GIDSCOMBE WAS SITTING (Mar. 1890)

**LEAD** SLUGS SHOT FROM SLINGS BY THE ANCIENT GREEKS IN BATTLE AS A CHALLENGE TO THE ENEMY, BORE THE GREEK WORD FOR *"TAKE THIS!"*

## THE STRANGEST SALVAGE OPERATION IN HISTORY

**A TUNNEL** 127 FEET DEEP AND 690 FEET LONG, WAS DUG BENEATH THE BOTTOM OF THE INDIAN OCEAN OFF PONDOLAND, So. AFRICA, IN 1921, IN A FUTILE ATTEMPT TO SALVAGE THE CARGO OF THE "GROSVENOR," WHICH SANK IN 1782 WITH *$10,000,000 WORTH OF GOLD, DIAMONDS, RUBIES AND EMERALDS.* THE EFFORT WAS ABANDONED WHEN THE TUNNEL WAS ONLY 30 FEET AWAY FROM THE SHIP'S POSITION

## THE MAN WHO COULDN'T BE HANGED

**JOSEPH SAMUELS**, SENTENCED TO DEATH FOR BURGLARY IN HOBART TOWN, AUSTRALIA, WAS GRANTED A REPRIEVE BY THE GOVERNOR AFTER *THE ROPE BROKE 3 TIMES*
(1803)

**A HATCHET** THAT SPELLS JEANNE, IN FRENCH, WAS IN THE 15th CENTURY --*THE SIGNATURE OF A FEMININE SOLDIER, JEANNE HACHETTE*

**THE HIGH SCHOOL** IN LAUGARVATN, ICELAND, DURING THE SUMMER RECESS *IS OPERATED AS A FIRST-RATE HOTEL*

A **WIDOW** IN THE **KAVATI TRIBE**, Africa, ALWAYS DRUMS LOUDLY ON THE GRAVE OF HER HUSBAND *— UNTIL SOMEONE MARRIES HER TO QUIET THE DIN*

THE **WETA** OF NEW ZEALAND, HAS A HEAD *HALF AS BIG AS ITS BODY*

**CLIMBING PLANTS** IN THE FOREST OF FRENCH GUIANA WIND SO TIGHTLY AROUND THE TRUNKS OF TREES *THEY DIG THROUGH THE BARK*

D.ᴿ **ANTOINE CLOT-BEY** (1793-1868) FRENCH CHIEF PHYSICIAN OF EGYPT FOR 26 YEARS WAS SO CONVINCED THAT THE PLAGUE WAS NOT CONTAGIOUS THAT 65 YEARS BEFORE THE TRUE NATURE OF THE DISEASE WAS DETERMINED *HE INJECTED HIMSELF WITH PLAGUE VIRUS* (1833)

MR. WOOD OF PLEASUREVILLE, KENTUCKY, IS A LUMBER DEALER

GERSAU, SWITZERLAND, WITH AN AREA OF 4 SQ. MILES, WAS FOR 413 YEARS AN INDEPENDENT REPUBLIC -- *THE SMALLEST REPUBLIC IN THE WORLD*

**THE STRANGEST SCHOOLING IN HISTORY**
THOMAS MURNER (1475-1537) A HUMANITIES PROFESSOR, ALWAYS TAUGHT HIS STUDENTS
*WHILE PLAYING CARDS WITH THEM-*
HE WAS A PROFESSOR AT THE UNIVERSITY OF CRACOW, POLAND, THE UNIVERSITY OF FREIBURG, GERMANY, THE UNIVERSITY OF LUCERNE, SWITZERLAND, AND THE UNIVERSITY OF TRIER, GERMANY

THE FEMALE LAMPYRID BEETLE of Rhodesia CARRIES BENEATH HER BODY A *GREEN LIGHT*

DWARF KOWHAIS, a New Zealand shrub, ARE ALWAYS HEMISPHERICAL--*AS IF THEY HAD BEEN TRIMMED BY A GARDENER*

BARS OF ROCK SALT ARE USED BY THE DANAKIL TRIBESMEN OF ETHIOPIA *AS MONEY—* A BAR A FOOT LONG IS WORTH ABOUT 60¢ AND IT CAN BE HALVED OR QUARTERED FOR CHANGE

JAMES "YANKEE" SULLIVAN AN EARLY 19th-CENTURY PRIZEFIGHTER ALWAYS FOUGHT *WITH AN AMERICAN FLAG BOUND AROUND HIS WAIST*

THE DUCHESS of BIRON (1770-1853) WHO MARRIED THE 85-YEAR-OLD DUKE WHEN SHE WAS 15, *DIED ON THE 153d ANNIVERSARY OF HIS BIRTH*

THE **MONUMENT TO THE BOLL WEEVIL** ENTERPRISE, ALABAMA,

A **MONUMENT** EXPRESSING THE TOWN'S GRATITUDE TO THE BOLL WEEVIL *WHICH FORCED THE LOCAL FARMERS TO CONVERT TO MORE-PROFITABLE PEANUT CROPS*

### EDWARD BIRKS
MANAGER OF THE GEORGE STREET BANK, IN SHEFFIELD, ENGLAND, DELIVERED A LECTURE ON BOTANY AT THE UNIVERSITY OF SHEFFIELD 3 TIMES A WEEK FOR 30 YEARS *BEFORE OPENING THE BANK FOR BUSINESS AT 9 A.M.*

A **COIN** MINTED BY LEONARD THURNEYSSER, A SWISS ALCHEMIST OF THE 16TH CENTURY, OUT OF A COMBINATION OF 7 DIFFERENT METALS *AS A TALISMAN AGAINST ACCIDENTS AND DISEASE*

### THE FISHING MONKEYS OF BORNEO
KRA MONKEYS, SO CALLED BECAUSE OF THE SOUND OF THEIR CRY, WADE THROUGH THE SHALLOW EDGES OF THE SEA *FISHING FOR CRABS*

THE **COVERED BRIDGE** IN PUTNEY, VT., ACTUALLY IS A SHOP *CREATED AS A REPLICA OF A HISTORIC COVERED SPAN*

THE **PALACE** of MUSTAPHA, RULER OF ALGIERS FROM 1799 TO 1806, HAD LOCKS ON EVERY DOOR *--BUT THEY COULD NOT BE SECURED FROM THE INSIDE* MUSTAPHA INSISTED HIS ONLY ENEMIES WERE IN HIS *OWN HOUSEHOLD*

A **WOMAN** OF THE NYAKUSA TRIBE OF AFRICA, UPON ENCOUNTERING ANY MAN, MUST *CROUCH ON THE GROUND AND VOICE THE GREETING: "YES, MY LORD?"*

**WOMEN** IN MEDIEVAL EUROPE FOUGHT MEN IN MORTAL COMBAT TO SETTLE JUDICIAL DISPUTES -- *BUT TO MAKE THE FIGHTS FAIR THE MEN WERE REQUIRED TO STAND IN A HOLE*

**HUTS** IN Brazzaville, Congo, HAVE REED DOORS THAT OPEN LIKE FANS SO HUMANS CAN SQUEEZE THROUGH--YET *THEY ARE A BARRIER AGAINST ANIMALS*

**KARL HUSS** (1761-1838) AN OFFICIAL AUSTRIAN HANGMAN PERFORMED HIS FIRST EXECUTION *AT THE AGE OF 15* WHEN CAPITAL PUNISHMENT WAS ABOLISHED IN 1787 HUSS WAS GRANTED A LICENSE TO PRACTICE MEDICINE

**"Pasha"**
AN 8-YEAR-OLD DRAY-
HORSE THAT PULLED
A BAKERY WAGON IN
WILHELMSHAVEN, GERMANY,
WAS ENTERED IN A
LOCAL RACE --*AND
WON IT EASILY*

**ARMANDE BEJART** (1645-1700)
MET FAMED FRENCH PLAYWRIGHT MOLIERE
WHEN SHE WAS ONLY 2 AND HE WAS 25
BUT SHE PUT HER ARMS AROUND HIS
NECK AND MURMURED:*"MON CHER
MARI" --"MY DEAR HUSBAND"*--
15 YEARS LATER THEY WERE MARRIED

A **HUMAN HAND**
CARVED IN
STONE BY AN
ABORIGINAL
INDIAN
AND FOUND
NEAR LAKE
KEJIMKOOJIK,
NOVA SCOTIA,
IS THE FIRST
INDICATION
THAT PRIMITIVES WERE
*AWARE OF THE IMPORTANCE
OF FINGERPRINTS*

A **MAGNIFICENT
SAILING SHIP**
56 FEET LONG, BUILT IN 1811
IN 27 DAYS FOR A VISIT BY
EMPEROR NAPOLEON I OF
FRANCE TO THE HARBOR OF
ANTWERP, WAS USED ONLY
*3 TIMES IN A PERIOD
OF 157 YEARS*

## AGRIPPA, d'AUBIGNE

(1552-1630) CELEBRATED AUTHOR AND HISTORIAN, KNEW LATIN, HEBREW AND GREEK *AT THE AGE OF 6*— HE WAS SENTENCED TO DEATH BY POLITICAL FOES 4 TIMES--THE FIRST TIME WHEN HE WAS 13-- BUT EACH TIME FLED IN TIME TO SAVE HIS LIFE

### SMALL FLIES
STEAL PIGGYBACK RIDES ON THE GIANT AFRICAN BEETLE

THE **CHURCH** of **SANTA MARIA** in **Assisi, Italy,** FOR 1,600 YEARS WAS A *ROMAN TEMPLE DEDICATED TO THE GODDESS MINERVA*

## NATIVES
of New Caledonia, in the Pacific, *FISH WITH BOW AND ARROW*

## THE STRANGE STONE BEDS OF THE SUDAN

RESTING PLACES CARVED IN THE SOLID CLIFFS OF THE SAHARA DESERT WITH STONE BALUSTRADES **TO ACCOMMODATE TRAVELERS** WHO WOULD OTHERWISE HAVE TO SPEND THE NIGHT ON THE HOT DESERT SAND

## THE LAUGH THAT SAVED A LIFE!

### LORD NORBURY
(1745-1831)

Chief Justice of Ireland, GIVEN ONLY A FEW HOURS TO LIVE SENT WORD TO A DYING FRIEND, **"IT WILL BE A DEAD HEAT BETWEEN US!"**

*HIS OWN JEST CAUSED LORD NORBURY TO LAUGH UPROARIOUSLY AND DOCTORS CREDITED THE JOKE WITH SAVING HIS LIFE*

## THE STATUE

OF A CHAINED WATCHDOG MOLDED FROM THE IMPRESSION MADE BY A DOG STRAINING TO ESCAPE THE **DESTRUCTION OF POMPEII** (79 A.D)

## THE STARRY FLOUNDER

HAS RAISED 5-POINTED STARS ON ONE SIDE OF ITS BODY *--AND BOTH EYES ON THE SAME SIDE OF ITS HEAD*

## WOOD HOMES

BUILT IN ST. OSWALD, AUSTRIA, WITHOUT NAILS AND ENCIRCLING A CENTRAL COURTYARD *ARE STILL STANDING AFTER 300 YEARS*

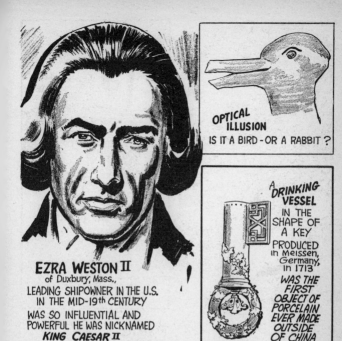

**OPTICAL ILLUSION**
IS IT A BIRD — OR A RABBIT ?

**EZRA WESTON II**
of Duxbury, Mass.,
LEADING SHIPOWNER IN THE U.S.
IN THE MID-19th CENTURY
WAS SO INFLUENTIAL AND
POWERFUL HE WAS NICKNAMED
*KING CAESAR II*

A *DRINKING VESSEL*
IN THE SHAPE OF A KEY
PRODUCED in Meissen,
Germany, in 1713
*WAS THE FIRST OBJECT OF PORCELAIN EVER MADE OUTSIDE OF CHINA*

THE **COWPUNCHER WHO COULDN'T STAND PROSPERITY**

*BOB WOMACK* A COWBOY WHO DISCOVERED GOLD IN POVERTY GULCH, COLO., IN 1890 *SOLD HIS CLAIM FOR $500 DURING A DRUNKEN SPREE—THE AREA YIELDED $800,000,000 WORTH OF GOLD*

**INDIAN TREE ANTS** CAPTURE AND SLAY FAR LARGER LONGICORN BEETLES BY ATTACKING FROM ALL SIDES AND *PINNING THE VICTIM'S ANTENNAE, LEGS AND WINGS TO THE GROUND*

## THE CHURCH OF PORT ARTHUR
in Australia
WAS DESIGNED AND BUILT BY
JAMES BLACKBURN -A PRISONER
IN THE PORT ARTHUR JAIL—
*HE WAS GIVEN A FULL PARDON
UPON ITS COMPLETION IN 1840*

The 10th EARL of COVENTRY
( 1838 - 1930 )
HELD HIS TITLE FOR
**86 YEARS**

## THE MOCK RUIN
BUILT AS THE BACKDROP OF THE STAGE
OF THE ANCIENT ROMAN THEATRE IN
Sabratha, Libya, Africa,
*IS THE MOST PERFECTLY PRESERVED
PART OF THE ENTIRE STRUCTURE*

A **BLIND AMPHIBIAN SALAMANDER** ( PROTEUS ANGUINUS )
FOUND IN SUBTERRANEAN CAVES IN CARNIOLA, YUGOSLAVIA,
*CAN EITHER LAY EGGS OR BEAR LIVE LARVA*

THE PUBLIC LIBRARY IN TRENTON, MISSOURI WAS BUILT WITH $50,000 DONATED BY JEWETT NORRIS --WHO WHILE LIVING IN THE COUNTY AS A YOUNG MAN HAD *EARNED EXACTLY THAT AMOUNT*

THE PAPER MONEY OF THE CITY OF ST. MAIXENT, FRANCE, WAS PRINTED IN 1791 *ON THE BACKS OF PLAYING CARDS*

QUEEN MARIE of Bavaria BOASTED THAT IN HER ENTIRE LIFETIME *SHE NEVER READ A BOOK*

THE OLD MAN OF THE MOUNTAIN near Portree, Scotland, NATURAL PROFILE FORMED BY A 1,200-FOOT-HIGH PEAK

THE **WEB** WOVEN BY THE RAGIOPE SPIDER OF GUIANA IS ALWAYS ORNAMENTED EXQUISITELY WITH *A GEOMETRICAL PETAL DESIGN*

**THE TOWERS OF NOTRE DAME** off the coast of New Caledonia, in the Pacific--*NATURAL ROCK FORMATION*

**C**HILDREN of the CHUKCHI TRIBE, IN ARCTIC SIBERIA, TO ENABLE THEIR PARENTS TO FIND THEM IN THE REGION'S FREQUENTLY DENSE FOGS *WEAR BELLS*

**THE CAVE OF CASTERET** in Spain, THE WORLD'S HIGHEST ICE CAVERN, CONTAINS A COLUMN OF FOSSIL ICE *UNCHANGED FOR 20,000 YEARS*

**BARON von TRENCK** (1726-1794) IMPRISONED FOR 10 YEARS BY KING FREDERICK THE GREAT OF PRUSSIA TO PREVENT HIM FROM ELOPING WITH THE KING'S SISTER, WROTE PLAYS, SONGS AND FAIRY TALES -- *IN BLOOD EXTRACTED FROM THE TIPS OF HIS FINGERS*

**BRACELETS** WORN BY INDIAN WOMEN OF THE LACANDON TRIBE, OF CHIAPAS, MEXICO -MADE FROM THE 8 CLAWS OF A PHEASANT

THE **ELEPHANT SHREW** NEVER CLOSES ITS EYES

A **LUCKY HIT** GENERAL BRUGÈRES MILITARY AIDE TO PRESIDENT JULES GRÈVY OF FRANCE, BECAUSE HE WAS ACCIDENTALLY WOUNDED BY THE PRESIDENT ON A HUNTING TRIP, WAS PROMOTED REPEATEDLY BY THE REMORSEFUL GRÈVY, AND *BECAME COMMANDER-IN-CHIEF OF THE FRENCH ARMY*

33

## THE CAVERN CONVENT

IN THE BUCSECS MOUNTAIN OF TRANSYLVANIA, RUMANIA, IS A MONASTERY IN A DEEP CAVE IN WHICH THE MONKS *OFTEN ARE SNOWED IN FOR MONTHS AT A TIME*

## POETIC JUSTICE

**AZZUBEIDI** (900-989) ARAB POET AND HISTORIAN WHO WAS MADE CHIEF JUSTICE OF SEVILLE AS A REWARD FOR COMPOSING A SINGLE POEM HONORING ITS MOORISH RULER, SULTAN AL HAKIM II, *MADE ALL HIS JUDICIAL DECISIONS IN VERSE*

## THE DWARF HIPPOPOTAMUS

FOUND IN Liberia

*IS ONLY 3 FEET HIGH*

## THE CRADLE THAT ROCKS

THE LITTLE HERMIT a hummingbird of Venezuela BUILDS A NEST OF FIBERS, DOWN AND FUNGUS AND HANGS IT FROM A LEAF WITH A STRONG SPIDER'S WEB *SO THAT IT SWAYS TO AND FRO WITH THE BREEZE*

A **MACHINE GUN** IS KNOWN TO THE ZULUS AS A "BY AND BY" BECAUSE WHEN THE FIRST ONE ARRIVED A EUROPEAN OFFERED TO EXPLAIN ITS USE "BY AND BY"

**GEORGE LIEBERWIRTH** of Zwickau, Germany, SPENT HIS SUMMER VACATIONS IN THE SAME HOTEL FOR **55** CONSECUTIVE YEARS

A **TOMBSTONE** IN THE CHURCHYARD OF SCHWÄBISH HALL, GERMANY, INDICATES THE CHARACTER OF THE DECEASED BY DEPICTING *A GLASS OF WINE, A BEAKER OF BEER AND DICE*

THE **DOLLAR** SIGN IN 16th-CENTURY PORTUGAL *WAS USED TO INDICATE "THOUSANDS" OF ANYTHING*

THE **WIDOW'S CAP**

A **HAT** MADE OF MUKA FIBER LACED WITH SEAWEED, WAS AWARDED BY THE MAORI TRIBESMEN OF NEW ZEALAND *TO WIDOWS WHOSE HUSBANDS FELL IN BATTLE* IT WAS CONSIDERED SUCH AN HONOR THAT IT HAD TO BE WORN NIGHT AND DAY UNTIL IT DISINTEGRATED

**S** WAS USED BY THE ETRUSCANS *AS BOTH A MULTIPLICATION SIGN (×) AND AS AN ADDITION SIGN (+)* WITH AN APOSTROPHE ADDED (S') IT WAS A LETTER IN THE ETRUSCAN ALPHABET *--PRONOUNCED AS M*

THE **FOUNTAIN** of **CHARLES V** in Besançon, France, FOR CENTURIES ON SUNDAYS AND HOLIDAYS *SPOUTED RED WINE*

A **TOMBSTONE** IN THE CEMETERY OF EYOUB, ISTANBUL, TURKEY, IS SHAPED LIKE A WINE GOBLET *TO EMPHASIZE THAT IT MARKS THE GRAVE OF A TEETOTALER*

**LAMPS** SHAPED LIKE A HUMAN FOOT WERE EXCHANGED BY THE ANCIENT ROMANS AS NEW-YEAR GIFTS IN THE BELIEF THEY WOULD *PREVENT MISSTEPS DURING THE COMING YEAR*

**MIMETUS SPIDER** of Guiana, So. America, TO DECEIVE SPIDER-HUNTING WASPS *HAS 2 PAINTED "EYES" ON ITS TAIL TO MAKE IT LOOK LIKE A LEAF HOPPER*

**NATIVES** OF RURAL AREAS OF THE ISLAND OF RHODES, GREECE, STILL WEAR BLACK MOURNING CLOTHES BECAUSE THEY FAILED TO DEFEAT THE TURKS *149 YEARS AGO*

**THE HOWLING CAVE** Forio Volastro, Italy, WHEN THE WIND BLOWS THROUGH IT *ECHOES WITH HUMANLIKE HOWLS AND SCREAMS*

**BULLFIGHTS** ARE STAGED BY THE BARA TRIBE OF MADAGASCAR TO TRAIN ITS YOUNG MEN IN THE ART OF *CATTLE RUSTLING*

**THE CANDELABRA PLANT** THE FLOWERS OF THE MARCGRAVIA PLANT OF SOUTH AMERICA *HANG LIKE AN INVERTED CANDELABRA—* IN THE CENTER ARE PITCHERS FILLED WITH NECTAR, WHICH ATTRACT INSECTS, WHICH IN TURN BRING THE BIRDS WHICH ASSURE POLLINATION OF THE PLANT

A **FARMER** in Minorca, Spain, PLOWING WITH A TEAM CONSISTING OF *A DONKEY AND A PIG*

**THE THOMAS EDISON MONUMENT**
IN THE IWASHIMIZU
SHRINE, IN KYOTO, JAPAN,
IS LOCATED IN THE
GROVE FROM WHICH
THE AMERICAN INVENTOR
*OBTAINED THE BAMBOO
USED AS A FILAMENT
IN HIS FIRST
INCANDESCENT LAMP*

**A FINGERPRINT**
AFFIXED TO A CHINESE
DEED OF SALE AS A
PROOF OF THE IDENTITY
OF THE OWNER IN 1839-
THE CHINESE HAVE
USED FINGERPRINTS
ON LEGAL DOCUMENTS
FOR MORE THAN
**1,000 YEARS**

ᕽast ᕽɪ-n ꞌadi-ꞌca iye-
kᵂeᵉ ᴛe - sitᕽᶜᶜ

**EPITAPH**
--ON THE TOMBSTONE OF HENRY
CHEE DODGE, TRIBAL LEADER AND
INTERPRETER OF THE NAVAJOS--
WHICH IS TRANSLATED TO READ:
*"MR. INTERPRETER RESTS HERE"*
Navajo Memorial Cemetery
Fort Defiance, Arizona

**EMPEROR CARACALLA**
( 188-217 )
OF ANCIENT ROME
WAS ACTUALLY
NAMED MARCUS
AURELIUS
ANTONINUS
BUT ADOPTED THE
NAME CARACALLA
*--GALLIC DESIGNATION
FOR THE HOODED TUNIC
HE MADE STYLISH*

A **13-STORY CHINESE PAGODA** WHICH HAS BECOME THE EMBLEM OF THE AMERICAN YENCHING UNIVERSITY, IN CHINA, ACTUALLY WAS BUILT IN 1926 *ONLY TO CONCEAL THE UNIVERSITY'S WATER TOWER*

THE **HUMAN CAMPAIGN POSTERS** *WOMEN* VOTING IN GUINEA IN 1958 ON A NEW CONSTITUTION THAT WOULD HAVE KEPT THEIR COUNTRY LINKED TO FRANCE, APPEARED AT THE POLLING PLACES IN BLOUSES ON WHICH THE WORD *"NON"* WAS REPEATED OVER AND OVER

THE **FIRST ART** A DESIGN FOUND IN A CAVE AT LIMEUL, FRANCE, WAS CREATED **30,000** YEARS AGO

*SIR* **WILLIAM JONES** (1746-1794) JUSTICE OF THE SUPREME COURT OF CALCUTTA, INDIA, THE FIRST ENGLISHMAN TO MASTER SANSKRIT, ALSO WAS EXPERT IN *40 OTHER LANGUAGES*

**PRINCE KAUNITZ**
the Austrian Chancellor,
WAS SO SENSITIVE TO DRAFTS IN
HIS OFFICE THAT HE ALWAYS WORKED
*WITH A GLASS BOWL
OVER HIS HEAD*

THE **GRAVE** OF FAMED
COMPOSER MOZART IN
ST. MARX CEMETERY, VIENNA,
*CONTAINS NO BODY—*
MOZART WAS BURIED IN A
MASS GRAVE, THE LOCATION
OF WHICH IS UNKNOWN

THE **HOME** of the HANGMAN OF NUREMBERG, GERMANY,
WAS A TOWER IN THE MIDDLE OF THE PEGNITZ RIVER BRIDGE
*--BECAUSE NO ONE WANTED TO LIVE NEAR A HANGMAN*

## TOMMASINA SPINOLA

WIFE OF BATTISTA SPINOLA, RULER OF GENOA, ITALY, WAS SO ARDENT AN ADMIRER OF KING LOUIS XII of France THAT WHEN SHE HEARD A FALSE RUMOR THAT THE FRENCH MONARCH HAD DIED *SHE SUCCUMBED OF A BROKEN HEART* (1505)

## THE STRANGE SCAPEGOATS OF MONGOLIA

A MONK of the Lawran Monastery IS DESIGNATED EACH YEAR AS "THE DEVIL" AND HE MUST VANISH FROM THE AREA FOREVER *-BEARING ALL THE SINS OF THE COMMUNITY*

## THE CHURCH OF SAN LORENZO IN MIRANDA, Rome,

WAS BUILT INSIDE THE COLUMNS OF AN ANCIENT PAGAN TEMPLE ERECTED BY EMPEROR ANTONINUS PIUS *1,800 YEARS AGO*

THE **MICHIGAN BUILDING** OF THE SAN FRANCISCO FAIR OF 1915, WAS PURCHASED BY A HOTEL MAN, DISMANTLED, MOVED TO A SITE NEAR PINO GRANDE, CALIF., AND RECONSTRUCTED AS THE DEER VIEW LODGE -- *BUT ITS OWNER DIED AND THE HOTEL NEVER OPENED*

**SEVERAL SWISS RAILROADS** DURING PERIODS OF COAL SHORTAGES DURING WORLD WAR II *GENERATED STEAM BY ELECTRICITY* WITH STEAM UNDER PRESSURE, THEY WERE ABLE TO OPERATE FOR HOURS ON NON-ELECTRIFIED TRACKS

**JONAS CATTELL** of Woodbury, N.J., TO DELIVER A LETTER TO CAPE MAY IN THE 18th CENTURY, WALKED 80 MILES IN A SINGLE DAY AND RETURNED THE NEXT DAY WITH THE ANSWER -- *WALKING 160 MILES IN 2 DAYS*

**EMPEROR CONSTANTINE the GREAT** RULED THE MIGHTY ROMAN EMPIRE **FOR 3 MONTHS AFTER HIS DEATH**

*THE EMPEROR'S EMBALMED BODY WAS PLACED IN THE THRONE ROOM AND COURT OFFICIALS CONTINUED TO CONSULT HIM DAILY UNTIL HIS SON AND SUCCESSOR RETURNED TO CONSTANTINOPLE*

**JUDGE JAMES BARLOW** AND **JUDGE JOHN BENAVIDES** TOTAL STRANGERS--WERE EACH MARRIED IN SAN ANTONIO, TEXAS, ON DEC. 22, 1951, BOTH HONEYMOONED IN MONTERREY, MEXICO -AND THE WIFE OF EACH MAN GAVE BIRTH TO A DAUGHTER ON THE SAME DAY -- JAN. 11, 1953 -- IN THE SAME HOSPITAL— BOTH MEN ARE NOW DISTRICT JUDGES IN SAN ANTONIO AND BOTH HAVE COURTROOMS ON THE 2ND FLOOR OF THE BEXAR COUNTY COURTHOUSE--

A **MEMORIAL** IN THE CHURCH OF ST. DENIS, FRANCE, *ENSHRINES THE HEART OF KING HENRI III*

43

A **BRIDGE** BUILT BY CHARLES COLLINS, of Collinsville, N.Y., IN 1878 AS AN EXACT DUPLICATE OF A BRIDGE IN SCOTLAND, COST HIM **$10,000** —YET THE ORIGINAL STRUCTURE WAS BUILT IN 1728 FOR **$600**

### GENERAL PIERRE DAUMESNIL
( 1777-1832 )
WHO HAD A LEG BLOWN OFF BY A SHELL WHILE SERVING UNDER NAPOLEON IN THE BATTLE OF WAGRAM, COMFORTED HIS GRIEVING ORDERLY BY JESTING :
*"WHAT ARE YOU WEEPING ABOUT? NOW YOU WILL HAVE ONLY ONE BOOT TO SHINE EACH MORNING!"*
( 1809 )

### THE RULER WHO BOUGHT HIS CROWN
*EMPEROR GALBA*
WHO RULED ROME FROM 68 TO 69 A.D. BECAME EMPEROR BY PAYING OFF EACH OF THE 4,000 SOLDIERS OF THE PALACE GUARD AND EACH OF THE 8,000 IN THE ROMAN GARRISON -- *A BRIBE THAT WOULD BE THE EQUIVALENT TODAY OF $686,040,000 !* HE WAS SLAIN BY HIS OWN SOLDIERS AFTER A REIGN OF 7 MONTHS BECAUSE *THEY FOUND HIM TO BE UNGENEROUS*

### ANTS
SEE IN THE DARKNESS BY MEANS OF **3 TINY EYES** IN THEIR FOREHEADS

**THE MAN WHO MADE A SAFE FLIGHT - *IN A BED!*** O.S. ELLWIN, OF LINDSBORG, KANSAS, WAS WHIRLED OUT OF HIS HOME BY A TORNADO AND DEPOSITED UNHARMED IN A FIELD **500** FEET AWAY - *STILL LYING IN HIS BED!* ( MAY 8, 1905 )

**THE SPIRE** OF THE CHURCH OF ST. MAURIZIO, in-CONIO, ITALY, **IS 300 YEARS OLDER THAN THE CHURCH** THE SPIRE WAS RETAINED FROM A CHURCH CONSTRUCTED ON THE SAME SITE IN THE 12th CENTURY

**A GIRL** OF THE PUNAN TRIBE OF BORNEO CELEBRATES HER MATURITY AT THE *AGE OF 3* AT THAT AGE SHE IS WEANED, CAN WEAR EARRINGS--AND *SMOKE A PIPE*

**ANTON NIEDERKIRCHER** POSTMASTER OF ZIRL, AUSTRIA, FROM 1790 UNTIL 1819 WAS SUCCEEDED IN THAT OFFICE BY HIS SON, HIS DAUGHTER, A GRANDSON, A GRANDDAUGHTER-IN-LAW AND A GREAT-GRANDSON *--THE SAME FAMILY FILLING THE POST FOR 148 YEARS*

HERE LIES A LITTLE MONKEY NAMED GOSCIO, MEANING "THE IDIOT" SO NAMED BY HUMANS HE TRIED TO IMITATE

EPITAPH IN GONDAR, ETHIOPIA, TO A MONKEY THAT DIED *OF ACUTE ALCOHOLISM*

**SERPENTS** IN PATAGONIA, SOUTH AMERICA, WHICH HAVE THE MARK OF A CROSS ON THEIR HEADS *ARE REVERED AND NEVER HARMED*

**SWEET POTATO MOUSE**

**HERODOTUS** (484-425 B.C.) THE GREEK FAMED AS THE "FATHER OF HISTORY" COULD EAT **20 POUNDS** OF MEAT AND DRINK **30 QUARTS** OF WINE *AT A SINGLE MEAL*

## EMPRESS ELIZABETH I

(1709-1762) of Russia
TOO LAZY TO DRESS AND
UNDRESS DURING THE LAST
4 YEARS OF HER LIFE
*WAS STITCHED INTO A
ROBE EACH MORNING
BY A SEAMSTRESS
--WHO RIPPED OUT THE
STITCHES EACH NIGHT*

## HELENA ANTONIA

AN 18-YEAR-OLD BEARDED LADY
VISITING GRAZ, AUSTRIA, FOR
A CARNIVAL, *RECEIVED 8
MARRIAGE PROPOSALS
IN A SINGLE DAY--*
SHE REJECTED THEM ALL
--AND NEVER RECEIVED
ANOTHER PROPOSAL DURING
HER ENTIRE LIFETIME

A **CHURCH** BUILT IN
ZINGST, GERMANY, IN 1856,
*WAS NOT PERMITTED TO HAVE
A BELFRY FOR 100 YEARS--*
IT WAS FEARED IT WOULD
CONFUSE SAILORS WHO USED AS
A NAVIGATION MARK THE BELFRY
OF A CHURCH IN NEARBY PREROV

47

**THE GATE** TO A FARM IN Boughton Monchelsea, England, IS TOPPED BY A STONE SHAPED LIKE A ROUND LOAF OF BREAD — *A WARNING TO MEDIEVAL BAKERS AGAINST CHEATING IN THE WEIGHT OF THEIR LOAVES*

## HUSSEIN MEZZO MORTO

A BARBARY PIRATE WHO BECAME RULER OF ALGIERS ADOPTED THE NAME "MEZZO MORTO" BECAUSE HE WAS CRITICALLY WOUNDED IN A BATTLE WITH THE SPANIARDS *–THE NAME MEANING "HALF DEAD"*

**FARM HOUSES** in the district of Orcières, France, HAVE THE LIVING QUARTERS ON THE GROUND FLOOR AND THE FLOORS ABOVE ARE USED, SUCCESSIVELY, AS *A STABLE A SHEEP MANGER, A GRANARY, AND A BEEHIVE*

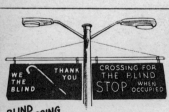

**BLIND CROSSING** *SIGN in Vancouver, Wash.,* NEAR THE WASHINGTON STATE SCHOOL FOR THE BLIND

48

THE **NEEDLE FISH** HAS JADE-GREEN BONES

THE **TOWER** of the CHURCH of St. LAMBERT in Munster, Germany, STILL FEATURES 3 CAGES CONSTRUCTED TO EXHIBIT *THE HEADS OF 3 CRIMINALS EXECUTED IN 1536*

**GOVERNOR BARDBAK** of Damascus NEVER SET DOWN HIS ROSARY, FINGERING IT CONSTANTLY DAY AND NIGHT- EVEN IN HIS SLEEP- *FOR 42 YEARS*

P. P. P. P. P. P.

THE LAST MESSAGE OF PIERRE PILLARD WHO WAS HANGED FOR TREASON, IN BRUSSELS, BELGIUM, IN 1667, WAS FINALLY DECIPHERED AS: "PRIEZ POUR PIERRE PILLARD PAUVRE PECHEUR PENDU" -*PRAY FOR PIERRE PILLARD POOR SINNER WHO WAS HANGED*

**THE POORHOUSE** of Exeter, England, WAS BUILT AS AN ACT OF ATONEMENT ON THE SPOT WHERE, IN 1531, A *HERETIC WAS BURNED AT THE STAKE*

49

A **COIN**
MINTED BY
KING SANCHO,
OF NAVARRA,
SPAIN,
A MEMORIAL
TO HIS SON,
FERNANDO, WHO
WAS KILLED IN
A HUNTING
ACCIDENT, READS:
*"RUIN OF THE
KINGDOM"*

**D**ANCING
**G**YPSIES
IN Tirana,
Albania,
PERFORM WITH
SUCH FRENZY
THAT ONLOOKERS
CUSTOMARILY PAY
THE DANCERS BY
PLACING COINS ON
THEIR FOREHEADS
*--WHICH ARE SO
COVERED WITH
PERSPIRATION THE
MONEY ADHERES
TO THEIR SKIN*

**PISTOLS** USED BY AMERICAN SAILORS
IN THE REVOLUTIONARY WAR
FOR BOARDING ENEMY VESSELS
*WERE EQUIPPED WITH BAYONETS*

THE
**STRANGEST**
**"WATCHDOGS"**
IN THE
WORLD
**LUZENDU**
A YOUTH OF
BAROTSELAND,
AFRICA,
HAVING
IMMUNIZED
HIMSELF
AGAINST
SCORPIONS
BY REPEATED
STINGS,
PROTECTED
HIS MONEY
*BY CARRYING
SCORPIONS
IN HIS
PURSE*

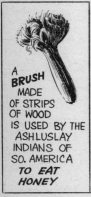

A
**BRUSH**
MADE
OF STRIPS
OF WOOD
IS USED BY THE
ASHLUSLAY
INDIANS OF
SO. AMERICA
*TO EAT
HONEY*

## BOAT BUILDERS

AMONG THE MAORI OF NEW ZEALAND, BECAUSE THEIR HANDS WERE SO REVERED, *NEVER TOUCHED FOOD*— THEY WERE FED BY YOUNG GIRLS FROM LONG FORKED STICKS

**ST. MICHAEL'S CHURCH** in Charleston, S.C., WHICH HAS HELD SERVICES REGULARLY SINCE 1681 *IS THE ONLY HUGUENOT CHURCH IN AMERICA*

## KLEMENS AINHIRN

SEXTON OF St. Leonard's Church, near Aussee, Austria, IS THE 7th GENERATION OF HIS FAMILY TO HOLD THAT POST— *276 YEARS OF CONTINUOUS SERVICE*

THE **CITY WALL** of Amelia, Italy, 2,800 FEET LONG, HAS NO CEMENT OR OTHER BINDER —YET IT HAS ENDURED FOR 3,400 YEARS

THE **VONEBIS**
OF SOUTH AMERICA
CREATE FESTIVAL MUSIC BY
*BLOWING INTO A CLAY JAR
WITH 2 WOODEN TUBES*

**THE TOWER OF BELENDA**
IN FINALE, ITALY,
WAS BUILT 600 YEARS AGO AS A
PRISON FOR A GIRL NAMED BELENDA,
*WHO PREFERRED DEATH IN A CELL
TO MARRIAGE TO HER KIDNAPER,
THE MARCHESE ALFONSO II*

Robert **OLDFIELD**
OF LONDON, ENGLAND,

MAINTENANCE MAN
IN A FACTORY,
PUT HIS BARE
HAND ON THE RAIL
OF AN ELECTRIC
CRANE -- AND
*SURVIVED A
CHARGE OF
415 VOLTS
AND 50
AMPERES*

A **NAIL FIDDLE**
USED IN GERMANY IN THE
18th CENTURY COMPRISED
A CIRCULAR FRAME
CONTAINING 99 IRON PINS
OF VARYING LENGTHS
*--WHICH WERE PLAYED
WITH A BOW*

**THE CITY OF THE DEAD**
Sicily

PANTALICA, A HIGH CLIFF
THAT SERVED THE ANCIENT SICILIANS
AS A CEMETERY, *IS HONEYCOMBED
WITH THOUSANDS OF GRAVES*—
IT CANNOT BE APPROACHED NOW
BECAUSE SWARMS OF BEES
HAVE HIVES IN THE CLIFF

**MAJOR WILLIAM CAIN**
A PROFESSOR OF MATHEMATICS
AT THE UNIVERSITY OF NO. CAROLINA
WAS COMMISSIONED AN OFFICER
IN THE ARMY OF THE CONFEDERACY
*AT THE AGE OF 14*

THE
**CHURCH** of **ST. MARTIN**
IN ALTENSTADT, GERMANY,
WAS BUILT OVER AND AROUND **AN ANCIENT ROMAN VILLA**

**JOHN STRYPE** (1643-1747) WAS PASTOR AT LOW LEYTON, ENGLAND, *FOR 66 YEARS*

THE **PALACE OF THE PRIORS** IN PERUGIA, ITALY, STILL DISPLAYS ON ITS FAÇADE A SYMBOL OF THE CITY'S SUCCESSFUL SIEGE OF SIENA IN 1358-- *A CHAIN BEARING THE KEYS AND BOLTS OF THE FORTRESS OF SIENA*

"THE SPHINX" AND "THE GREAT PYRAMID" NEAR MAGHARA, IN THE SINAI DESERT, *BOTH NATURAL ROCK FORMATIONS*

**THE MOST SENTIMENTAL MEMORIAL TO A HORSE** A **MOSAIC** IN THE FLOOR OF A ROMAN VILLA NEAR CONSTANTINE, ALGERIA, INSTALLED MORE THAN 1,900 YEARS AGO, DEPICTS THE OWNER'S HORSE AND READS: "WHETHER YOU WIN OR NOT, WE LOVE YOU, POLIDOXUS"

**THE CHURCH OF ST. ANNE**
IN GÖSTING, AUSTRIA,
*ORIGINALLY WAS A BEER*
*HALL FOR 110 YEARS*

THE **BUTCHER !**
**AHMAD PASHA,** WHO RULED
SYRIA FROM 1780 TO 1804,
SUSPECTING THAT ONE OF HIS
37 WIVES HAD BEEN UNFAITHFUL
*HAD ALL 37 OF THEM*
*CREMATED TOGETHER*

THE **MALE**
**PATAGONIAN**
**FROG**
( *Rhinoderma*
*darwini* )
HATCHES THE FEMALE'S
EGGS IN HIS LARYNX
*-AFTER SWALLOWING*
*THEM*

THE **POOL** CONSTRUCTED IN
KIRSTENBOSCH, NEAR CAPE TOWN, S.A.,
BY COLONEL **BIRD,**
DEPUTY COLONIAL SECRETARY,
*IS SHAPED LIKE A BIRD*

55

THE **ANIMAL THAT WALKS ON CASTANETS**
THE ELAND, TO ENABLE IT TO WALK ON DESERT SAND, HAS HOOVES THAT SPREAD WITH EACH STEP-- AND ITS TOES SNAP TOGETHER WITH THE SOUND OF CASTANETS

**TWIN GIRLS** BORN IN THE ASHANTI TRIBE, AFRICA, WHEN THEY GROW UP MUST *BOTH MARRY THE TRIBE'S CHIEF*

A **7-TOED CAT** GAVE BIRTH TO FOUR **7-TOED KITTENS** OWNED BY MRS. NELSON R. HOISTION Felts Mills, N.Y.

**NATIVES** on the island of Raroia, in the South Pacific, *FISH WITH HUNTING DOGS* THE DOGS SWIM OUT AT HIGH TIDE AND DRIVE THE FISH TO WHERE THE NATIVES CAN HARPOON THEM

**THE 4 CILEK BROTHERS** of Iowa City, Iowa,
MIKE, 21 -- NICK, 16 -- GREG, 14 --AND DAN, 13 --
EACH PLAYED QUARTERBACK ON A DIFFERENT SCHOOL TEAM AND
IN 4 GAMES PLAYED IN A SINGLE WEEK-END
*EACH LED HIS TEAM TO VICTORY*

**DOLOMITE FLAX**
A PLANT SURVIVING FROM
THE CENOZOIC GEOLOGICAL
PERIOD OF 20,000,000
YEARS AGO, *NOW GROWS
NOWHERE ELSE IN THE
WORLD BUT ON ONE HILL-
TOP NEAR BUDAPEST, HUNGARY*

**ARNOLD DOBLER**
THE GRAVEDIGGER
of Neustadt, Germany, FOR **38**
YEARS, ALWAYS DUG A NEW GRAVE
*24 HOURS BEFORE THE DEATH
OF A FELLOW PARISHIONER.*
DOBLER INSISTED HE ALWAYS
SAW THE NEXT OCCUPANT OF
HIS CEMETERY IN A DREAM--
**BEFORE THE VICTIM'S DEATH!**

THE **CORPSE** OF A CHIEF ON NEW IRELAND, AN ISLAND IN THE PACIFIC, IS DRESSED IN FINERY, ADORNED WITH BRACELETS AND A FLOWER BEHIND EACH EAR, THEN CARRIED THROUGH THE VILLAGE *SEATED IN A BAMBOO CHAIR*

THE **HAIRY FROG** of Africa **IS COVERED WITH FUR**

(Trichobatrachus robustus)

M.E. KELLOGG 1882 DIED A NATURAL DEATH

EPITAPH IN BOOTHILL CEMETERY TOMBSTONE, ARIZONA

## TITUS POMPONIUS ATTICUS

(110-33 B.C.) A WEALTHY ROMAN WHO REACHED THE AGE OF 77 WITHOUT EVER BEING ILL, WAS SO TERRIFIED OF OLD AGE *THAT HE COMMITTED SUICIDE BY REFUSING TO EAT OR DRINK*

THE **CASTLE OF VISCHERING,** IN GERMANY, HAS BEEN OWNED BY THE DROSTE FAMILY *CONTINUOUSLY FOR 699 YEARS*

## THE GREATEST BOOK THIEF IN HISTORY

Count Libri (1803-1869) 25-YEAR-OLD PROFESSOR OF MATHEMATICS AT THE UNIVERSITY of PISA, ITALY, WAS APPOINTED INSPECTOR GENERAL OF ALL FRENCH LIBRARIES AND STOLE SO MANY RARE BOOKS THAT ALTHOUGH HE HAD TO FLEE TO ENGLAND TO ESCAPE A PRISON SENTENCE HE WAS WEALTHY ALL THE REST OF HIS LIFE *—SELLING OFF HIS STOLEN VOLUMES ONE BY ONE--* HIS FAMILY NAME, LIBRI, IS LATIN FOR "BOOKS"

THE **KNEEPADS** USED BY TRIBAL DANCERS OF SOUTH MALLICOLO, IN THE NEW HEBRIDES, *WERE FACE MASKS WHICH HAD A HUMAN BONE THROUGH THE NOSTRILS AND HAIR MADE OF SPIDER WEBS*

THE **NEST** OF THE MASON WASP OF INDIA COMPRISES A CLUSTER OF OVAL POTS MADE *OF FINE MUD AND A LAYER OF RESIN*

59

**DR. J. RUSH**, of Concordia, Missouri, AFTER 7 BUILDINGS HAD BEEN SET ON FIRE BY AN ARSONIST, ORGANIZED A PRAYER MEETING TO ASK DIVINE HELP IN UNMASKING THE CULPRIT *THE NEXT DAY DR. RUSH HIMSELF WAS EXPOSED AS THE CRIMINAL AND WAS CONVICTED AND HANGED* (1874)

THE **BELFRY** OF THE CHURCH OF ST. PETER, IN BRUSSELS, BELGIUM, WAS STARTED IN 1517 *--BUT WAS LEFT UNCOMPLETED FOR 381 YEARS*

THE **MACARTHUR HOUSE** IN Parramatta, Australia, WHICH WAS BUILT IN 1793, *IS AUSTRALIA'S OLDEST HOME*

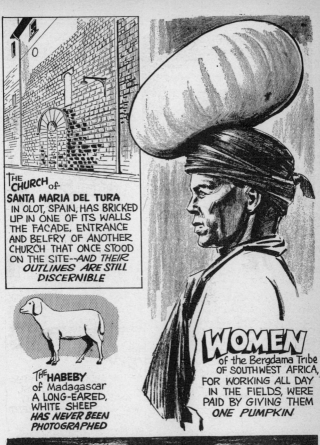

THE **CHURCH** of **SANTA MARIA DEL TURA** IN OLOT, SPAIN, HAS BRICKED UP IN ONE OF ITS WALLS THE FACADE, ENTRANCE AND BELFRY OF ANOTHER CHURCH THAT ONCE STOOD ON THE SITE--*AND THEIR OUTLINES ARE STILL DISCERNIBLE*

THE **HABEBY** of Madagascar A LONG-EARED, WHITE SHEEP *HAS NEVER BEEN PHOTOGRAPHED*

**WOMEN** of the Bergdama Tribe OF SOUTHWEST AFRICA, FOR WORKING ALL DAY IN THE FIELDS, WERE PAID BY GIVING THEM *ONE PUMPKIN*

**THE SLEEPING GIANT** HELENA, MONTANA NATURAL STONE FORMATION

## CLAUDE-LOUIS GABRIEL

( 1697-1775 )
WAS A LICENSED ATTORNEY IN METZ, FRANCE, AND ALREADY A CELEBRATED COURTROOM ORATOR *AT THE AGE OF 16*

**THE FIRST BABY CARRIAGE** WAS CONSTRUCTED IN NEW YORK BY CHARLES BURTON IN **1848**

**Q.** WHICH STATE HAS THE LARGEST NUMBER OF TELEPHONE CALLS ANNUALLY IN PROPORTION TO ITS POPULATION?

**A.** *ALASKA, WITH 630 CALLS PER PERSON. HAWAII RANKS NEXT WITH 530. ALL THE REST OF THE U.S. AVERAGES ONLY 426 CALLS PER PERSON.*

**THE RICE-CHERRY HOUSE** In Houston, Texas, SINCE ITS CONSTRUCTION IN 1850, HAS BEEN MOVED TO DIFFERENT SITES **3 TIMES** -- IN 1897 IT WAS GIVEN TO A PURCHASER FOR $25, *THE AMOUNT HE HAD OFFERED FOR THE FRONT DOOR*

### A HOLLOW OAK TREE

NEAR ERLE, GERMANY, WHICH IS MORE THAN 1,000 YEARS OLD, WAS FOR CENTURIES THE SEAT OF A SECRET TRIBUNAL IN WHICH *HOODED JUSTICES METED OUT SENTENCES*

**"TABATHA"** A CAT WITH **28 TOES**

### THE BEGUM LIAQUAT KHAN

WIDOW OF AN ASSASSINATED PRIME MINISTER OF PAKISTAN WAS APPOINTED PAKISTANI AMBASSADOR TO THE NETHERLANDS IN 1954 --*THE FIRST WOMAN AMBASSADOR OF A MOSLEM COUNTRY*

### BLACK TOMMY

A HORSE ENTERED IN THE BRITISH DERBY IN 1857, WAS SUCH A FAVORITE THAT ITS OWNER, NAMED DRINKALD, *BET $100,000 ON HIM AGAINST A COAT, VEST AND HAT*-- BLACK TOMMY LOST AND HIS OWNER PAID OFF

### TRACTORS

ORIGINALLY WERE 2 SMALL RODS MADE OF DIFFERENT METALS --INVENTED BY DR. ELISHA PERKINS, OF NORWICH, CONN, *AS A "CURE" FOR RHEUMATISM*

**HUTS** OF THE CHARI TRIBESMEN OF CENTRAL AFRICA ARE BUILT AROUND A LARGE GOURD TREE, THE DENSE FOLIAGE OF WHICH KEEPS THE HOMES *BOTH DRY AND COOL*

THE **LIGHT-FINGERED BANKER MONTAGUE NORMAN** [1871-1950] GOVERNOR OF THE BANK OF ENGLAND FOR **24** YEARS *HAD LUMINOUS FINGERS THAT GLOWED IN THE DARK*

## THE JOSEPH CANAL

WHICH EXTENDS 270 MILES THROUGH UPPER EGYPT--IRRIGATING AN AREA FAMED FOR ITS ROSES--*IS STILL IN USE 3,700 YEARS AFTER ITS CONSTRUCTION BY THE BIBLICAL JOSEPH*

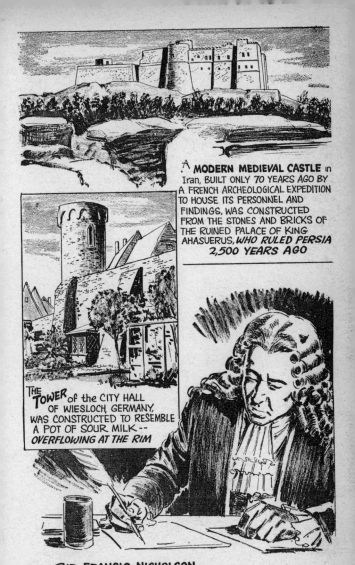

A **MODERN MEDIEVAL CASTLE** in Iran, BUILT ONLY 70 YEARS AGO BY A FRENCH ARCHEOLOGICAL EXPEDITION TO HOUSE ITS PERSONNEL AND FINDINGS, WAS CONSTRUCTED FROM THE STONES AND BRICKS OF THE RUINED PALACE OF KING AHASUERUS, *WHO RULED PERSIA 2,500 YEARS AGO*

THE **TOWER** of the CITY HALL OF WIESLOCH, GERMANY, WAS CONSTRUCTED TO RESEMBLE A POT OF SOUR MILK -- *OVERFLOWING AT THE RIM*

**SIR FRANCIS NICHOLSON**
( 1655-1728 ) FOUNDED **28** CHURCHES AND *SERVED SUCCESSIVELY AS ROYAL GOVERNOR OF VIRGINIA, MARYLAND, SO. CAROLINA AND NOVA SCOTIA AND LIEUT. GOV. OF NEW YORK*

## CEMETERIES
IN HAITI OFTEN ARE DESIGNED LIKE MINIATURE CITIES-- *WITH EACH GRAVESTONE RESEMBLING A SMALL HOUSE* NICHES DOUBLE AS WINDOWS AND AS DEPOSITORIES FOR CHARITABLE CONTRIBUTIONS

### THE OLD SOLDIER
**THE EARL OF LUCAN** (1800-1888) SERVED IN THE BRITISH ARMY FOR **72** YEARS AND WAS MADE A FIELD MARSHAL *AT THE AGE OF 87*

### THE BASHFUL BARD
*NICHOLAS FORMÉ* (1567-1638) THE CELEBRATED FRENCH COMPOSER, UPON HEARING HIS OWN COMPOSITIONS SUNG, *ALWAYS FAINTED*

### DR. CARLOS P. ROMULO
FOREIGN SECRETARY OF THE PHILIPPINES, *WAS AWARDED HIS 70TH HONORARY ACADEMIC DEGREE AT THE AGE OF 70*

**TEMPLE**
A LAMINATED ROCK
FORMATION ON THE
SHORE OF THE
COLORADO RIVER

**SCHNUTI PIUS** of GERSAU, Switzerland, IN SUMMER AND WINTER ALWAYS WORE **3 VESTS AND 5 SHIRTS**

**THE LAST LAUGH!**
HA HA CEMETERY
LOCATED IN ALBERT
COUNTY, New Brunswick

**THE ALBATROSS**
HAS THE LONGEST INCUBATION
PERIOD IN NATURE--THE
PARENTS TAKING TURNS
SITTING ON THE EGG FOR
*AS LONG AS 80 DAYS*

**THE ZEBRA FINCH**
OF AUSTRALIA
HATCHES ITS EGGS IN
*ONLY 11 DAYS*

67

AN **ESTATE** OF 190 ACRES IN WHAT IS NOW THE CITY OF SYDNEY, AUSTRALIA, WAS GRANTED IN 1815 TO CAPT. JOHN PIPER BY THE GOVERNOR BECAUSE *HE WAS GALLANT ENOUGH TO LEAVE THE BEACH WHEN HE FOUND THAT THE GOVERNOR'S WIFE WAS BATHING THERE*

**SIR MEIRING BECK** PHYSICIAN AND SENATOR in Capetown, So. Africa, ALL HIS LIFE INSISTED THAT MEMBERS OF HIS HOUSEHOLD *SPEAK ONLY ENGLISH EACH MONDAY, AFRIKAANS ON TUESDAY, FRENCH ON WEDNESDAY, GERMAN ON THURSDAY AND ITALIAN ON FRIDAY*

**A BASEBALL GAME** BETWEEN 2 MAINE HIGH SCHOOLS--OXFORD HILLS AND MORSE--ENDED IN A 1 TO 0 VICTORY FOR OXFORD HILLS, *ONLY AFTER 20 INNINGS OF PLAY*

**ELEPHANT TAILS** ONCE WERE USED IN ANGOLA, PORTUGUESE W. AFRICA, *AS MONEY*

THE **OLDEST WOODEN IMPLEMENT** A WOOD PADDLE FOUND IN DUVENSEE, GERMANY, WAS CARVED *9,000 YEARS AGO*

THE **WEATHERMAN WHO NEVER HEARS A KIND WORD** WOMEN of the Rajbansi Tribe of India, PERFORMING A RAIN DANCE AROUND A STATUE OF THEIR RAIN GOD, HUDUM DEO, HURL INSULTS AT THE STATUE CONSTANTLY IN THE BELIEF HE *WILL CREATE RAIN JUST TO END THE TORRENT OF ABUSE*

**ZACHARIAH D. BLACKISTONE** OF WASHINGTON, D.C., STILL PLAYS TOURNAMENT GOLF *AT THE AGE OF 99*

**VANE CASTLE** in Angus, Scotland, IS A MEMORIAL TO THE YOUNGEST SON OF ITS BUILDER, WHO LEARNED HIS CHILD HAD BEEN DROWNED NEARBY, AND CRIED, *"IT IS ALL IN VAIN!"*

THE **CORONATION STAMPS** OF SOUTH AFRICA WERE ISSUED IN 1936 IN PAIRS -- *ONE IN ENGLISH AND THE OTHER IN AFRIKAANS*

THE MOST AMAZING SHIP RACE IN HISTORY! THE S.S. LUFRA AND THE WAGOOLA RACED FROM HOBART, TASMANIA, TO LONDON, ENGLAND --*A DISTANCE OF 11,000 MILES*--AND *FINISHED IN A DEAD HEAT!* THEY SAILED FROM HOBART ON JULY 26, 1876 AND REACHED LONDON ON OCT 25th JUST 7 MINUTES APART --SO THE 91-DAY RACE WAS OFFICIALLY PRONOUNCED A TIE

**ALBERT FROIDEVAUX** OF LAUSANNE, SWITZERLAND, A QUADRUPLE AMPUTEE, TO PREPARE HIS BIOGRAPHY FOR PUBLICATION *TYPED THE ENTIRE MANUSCRIPT HIMSELF*

THE **FLYCATCHERS** OF PANAMA ARE THE ONLY SPECIES OF BIRDS *IN WHICH THE FEMALES FIGHT FOR THE FAVOR OF THE MALE*

A **SPIDER** NEVER GETS STUCK ON THE STICKY THREADS OF ITS WEB BECAUSE IT KEEPS ITS OWN BODY *CONSTANTLY OILED*

70

### THE SUICIDE STONE

A ROCK IN GUÉNIN, FRANCE, HOLLOWED OUT TO FIT A HUMAN HEAD, WAS LONG USED BY NATIVES TIRED OF LIFE WHO WOULD PERSUADE AN OBLIGING NEIGHBOR TO **CLUB THEM TO DEATH**

HE PRACTICED KINDNESS AND CHARITY AS STEALTHILY AS SOME MEN COMMIT CRIMES

*Epitaph* TO BENJAMIN SAXON STORY, A PHILANTHROPIST, IN Metairie Cemetery, New Orleans, La.

THE **KATARA** A SCULPTURED FIGURE OF WOOD, GUARDS NATIVE HUTS IN NEW CALEDONIA AND WHEN DEATH OCCURS *ITS NOSE IS BROKEN AS PUNISHMENT FOR ITS LACK OF VIGILANCE*

THE **JUDGE** OF THE M'CHOUNECHE TRIBE OF THE AURES REGION OF ALGERIA AS HIS EMBLEM OF OFFICE *WEARS A 210-YEAR-OLD HAT DECORATED WITH ASTROLOGICAL SIGNS AND THE STAR OF DAVID*

71

THE **6** **GUENTER BROTHERS**
of Butler, N.J.,
ALL SERVED AS CITY FIREMEN
--*PUTTING IN A TOTAL OF 161 YEARS
FIGHTING FIRES*

**MATERNITY ROCK**, Locronan, France,
A STONE ON WHICH CHILDLESS WOMEN SIT
IN THE BELIEF IT WILL ASSURE THEM
*A SON OR DAUGHTER WITHIN A YEAR*

THE
**ENGINEERING BAT**
of Panama WEAKENS
THE RIBS OF PALM
LEAVES SO THAT THE
LEAVES DROOP OVER
*TO CREATE A COOL,
WATERPROOF REFUGE*

A **LIGHT BULB**
IN THE VAULT OF A SAVINGS
AND LOAN ASSOCIATION IN
LAMAR, COLO., HAS BEEN
BURNING THROUGHOUT
THE BUSINESS DAY,
5 DAYS A WEEK,
*FOR 57 YEARS*

**BENOIT
FOURNEYRON**
WAS
APPOINTED
PROFESSOR OF
MATHEMATICS
AT THE MINING
ACADEMY OF
ST. ETIENNE,
FRANCE,
*AT THE AGE
OF 16*

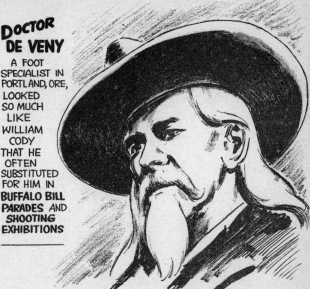

**DOCTOR DE VENY** A FOOT SPECIALIST IN PORTLAND, ORE, LOOKED SO MUCH LIKE WILLIAM CODY THAT HE OFTEN SUBSTITUTED FOR HIM IN **BUFFALO BILL PARADES** AND **SHOOTING EXHIBITIONS**

THE **TIGRE du BENGAL**, A FRENCH PRIVATEER, ESCAPED CAPTURE BY A BRITISH WAR VESSEL OFF ZANZIBAR IN 1805 BY LAUNCHING A DOZEN BARRELS IN THE ROUGH WATER --*AND PUTTING INTO EACH BARREL 2 ENGLISH PRISONERS*-- THE CAPTAIN OF THE BRITISH WARSHIP HAD TO PICK UP THE PRISONERS--AND FOUND EACH PAIR HAD BEEN PROVIDED WITH A BOTTLE OF WINE AND A DECK OF PLAYING CARDS

**THE FEMALE YELLOW BILLED TROPIC BIRD** OF SOUTH AMERICA DOES ALL THE LABOR OF BUILDING THE NEST —WHILE THE MALE SITS ON A NEARBY BRANCH AND SINGS ENCOURAGEMENT

## WOMEN

of the Gwari Tribe of Northern Nigeria CARRY TO MARKET GREAT BUNDLES OF FIREWOOD WEIGHING **100** POUNDS —AND OFTEN CARRY THEIR BABIES IN SLINGS BENEATH THE LOAD THE WOMEN OFTEN TRAVEL AS FAR AS **15** MILES WITH SUCH LOADS WHICH ARE TWICE AS HEAVY AS THOSE LEGALLY PERMITTED MALE PORTERS

### THE APARTMENT HOUSE NESTS

THE ICARIAN WASP BUILDS NESTS OF WOOD FIBERS WHICH IT SUSPENDS FROM THE BRANCH OF A TREE —ALWAYS CONSTRUCTING A SERIES OF NESTS WITH EXACTLY THE SAME CIRCUMFERENCE

THE **COLOR** ON A BUTTERFLY'S WINGS IS FAST, YET A MOTH'S COLORS ALWAYS FADE

THE **ALTAR** OF THE CHURCH OF THE CATACOMB, in Saragossa, Spain, ON WHICH REGULAR SERVICES ARE HELD DAILY, IS A COFFIN CONTAINING THE BONES OF EARLY CHRISTIAN MARTYRS

**THE ROOT OF ALL EVIL!**
THE CURRENCY OF THE PIAROA INDIANS OF COLOMBIA AND VENEZUELA, IS CURARE-- *THE DEADLY POISON USED IN BLOWGUNS*

THAT'S THE WAY THE BALL BOUNCES!

**BEDFORD HIGH SCHOOL** in Bedford, Iowa, IN ITS 1969-1970 SEASON HAD A BASKETBALL TEAM THAT *WON EVERY GAME* AND A FOOTBALL TEAM THAT *LOST EVERY GAME*

THE REV. **REUBEN SEIDERS** of Boston, Mass., AFTER MARRYING MISS SUSAN AUSTIN IN 1837 *ADOPTED HIS WIFE'S MAIDEN NAME*-- HE BECAME KNOWN AS THE REV. REUBEN AUSTIN

**DENVER** WHICH CALLS ITSELF "THE MILE HIGH CITY" JUSTIFIES THAT NAME BECAUSE *THE 15th STEP OF THE COLORADO STATE CAPITOL IS EXACTLY 5,280 FEET ABOVE SEA LEVEL*

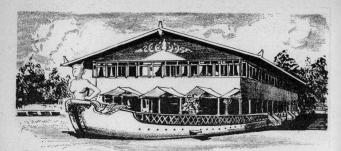

THE **KINNAREENAVA RESTAURANT** IN BANGKOK, THAILAND, IS LOCATED ON A LAKE IN THE THAI CAPITAL'S PARK -- ON *A REPLICA OF AN ANCIENT ROYAL BARGE*

THE **CHAPEL** IN THE CONVENT OF SAO FRANCISCO, IN EVORA, PORTUGAL, HAS WALLS AND COLUMNS THAT ARE COVERED WITH *HUMAN BONES*

# KING FIROZ II

WHO RULED PERSIA FROM 458 TO 484 WAS SLAIN IN A BATTLE IN WHICH *29 OF HIS SONS ALSO DIED !*

THE **NEST** OF THE SPARASSUS SPIDER OF INDIA IS FORMED BY TWISTING BLADES OF GRASS INTO AN ARTISTIC SPIRAL

### THE RIVER THAT WAS CONDEMNED FOR TREASON!

### THE JAIK RIVER
Russia

ACCUSED OF PERMITTING A REBEL TO CROSS IT, WAS ORDERED TO STAND TRIAL BY EMPRESS CATHERINE THE GREAT **AND CONDEMNED TO DEATH!** *THE SENTENCE WAS CARRIED OUT BY RENAMING IT THE URAL RIVER* (1775)

### THE CORPSE THAT RULED ETHIOPIA

### EMPEROR MENELIK II
DIED ON SEPT. 10, 1911

BUT FOR 2 YEARS, 3 MONTHS AND 2 DAYS *HE WAS STILL CONSIDERED THE REIGNING MONARCH BY ALL HIS SUBJECTS*

**JOHN DUDENEY** (1782-1852) of South Downs, England, NEVER ATTENDED SCHOOL, BUT WHILE WORKING AS A SHEPHERD *TAUGHT HIMSELF FRENCH, HEBREW, ASTRONOMY and MATHEMATICS* HE BECAME SO SCHOLARLY THAT HE WAS APPOINTED A SCHOOLMASTER

**THE CHORTEN** OF **TASSIDING, India,** IS CONSIDERED SO SACRED *THAT THE MERE SIGHT OF IT* **CLEANSES A MAN OF ALL SIN**

**ALEXANDER McGILLIVRAY** of Dalcrombie, Scotland, WHO WAS SLAIN IN THE BATTLE OF CULLODEN AFTER HAVING KILLED **9** ENEMY SOLDIERS WITH HIS SWORD, HAD TO BE BURIED WITH THE WEAPON *—BECAUSE HIS HAND HAD BECOME SO SWOLLEN IT COULD NOT BE WITHDRAWN FROM THE HILT* (April 16, 1746)

**JEAN-MICHEL MOREAU** (1741 - 1814) WAS A COLLEGE PROFESSOR IN THE ACADEMY OF FINE ARTS in St. Petersburg, Russia, *AT THE AGE OF* **17**

AN **ELABORATE LAMP** FOUND IN THE TOMB OF KING TUT, in Egypt, WAS CARVED FROM A *SINGLE BLOCK OF ALABASTER*

THE **CATHEDRAL** of **ETCHMIADZYN** ( Armenia) ERECTED IN 303 BY KING TIRIDATES AND STILL STANDING AFTER 1,667 YEARS *WAS THE FIRST STRUCTURE TO BE TOPPED BY A CROSS*

ANY **LEGISLATOR** in Locri, Ancient Greece, WHO PROPOSED A NEW LAW WAS COMPELLED TO APPEAR WITH A **NOOSE AROUND HIS NECK!**

*HE WAS STRANGLED IF THE MEASURE WAS VETOED — NO LAWS WERE INTRODUCED FOR 200 YEARS*

THE **ROCKING** STONE of **AMALIENDORF**, Austria, A BOULDER 100 FEET HIGH SO PRECARIOUSLY BALANCED *IT CAN BE MOVED BY A CHILD*

THE **WHALE** AND THE **KANGAROO RAT** *ARE THE ONLY MAMMALS IN ALL NATURE THAT HAVE 6 OF THEIR 7 NECK VERTEBRAE FUSED TOGETHER*

79

THE *ABIPONE* INDIANS of Paraguay WORE A CROSS CUT INTO THEIR FOREHEADS AS A SACRED SYMBOL *LONG BEFORE COLUMBUS DISCOVERED THE NEW WORLD*

**THE PUBLIC CLOCK** in the Borghese Park, Rome, Italy, *IS RUN SOLELY ON WATER POWER*

A **MAPLE BOARD** BEARING THE NATURAL SCULPTURE OF A *BULL'S HEAD*

THE SIBELIUS MONUMENT in Helsinki, Finland, IS SHAPED LIKE THE PIPES OF AN ORGAN -- *TO SYMBOLIZE COMPOSER JEAN SIBELIUS' BRILLIANCE*

**INDIAN CORN** AFTER BEING HARVESTED BY NOSU TRIBESMEN OF THE YANGTZE VALLEY, IN CHINA, IS KEPT OUT OF THE REACH OF CATTLE BY *STACKING IT IN THE TOPS OF TREES*

A **7-NO-TRUMP HAND** DEALT IN A CONTRACT BRIDGE GAME TO NOEL DANT, OF EDMONTON, ALBERTA

**SALT** IN THE WESTERN SUDAN, AFRICA, IS SOLD *"BY THE STRAW"*— THE SALT IS CRYSTALLIZED AROUND THE STRAW AND SOLD A DOZEN AT A TIME

**COINS** USED IN 18TH CENTURY MEXICO WERE MINTED IN THE SHAPE OF LEAVES

**FRANCESCO FRACANZANI** ( 1612-1657 ) A SUCCESSFUL ITALIAN PAINTER, WAS SENTENCED TO BE HANGED AS A HIGHWAYMAN -BUT A PRISON GUARD WHO ADMIRED HIS ART MADE IT POSSIBLE FOR HIM TO CHEAT THE GALLOWS WITH A VIAL OF POISON

## GEORGE W. RICHMANN (1711-1753)

SWEDISH PHYSICIST EMPLOYED BY THE ACADEMY OF SCIENCES, IN ST. PETERSBURG, RUSSIA, ATTEMPTED TO DUPLICATE BENJAMIN FRANKLIN'S EXPERIMENTS WITH ELECTRICITY DURING A THUNDERSTORM, BUT WAS KILLED WHEN A BALL OF FIRE LEAPED FROM AN IRON BAR *AND BURST AGAINST HIS FOREHEAD*

THE **ENTRANCE** TO THE SDRAGONATO CAVE, NEAR BONIFACIO, ON THE ISLAND OF CORSICA *IS SHAPED LIKE THE OUTLINE OF CORSICA*

## THE TORQUE

A TWISTED CORD WORN ON THE CHEST BY THE SOLDIERS OF ANCIENT ROME *WAS THE FIRST MILITARY DECORATION FOR VALOR*

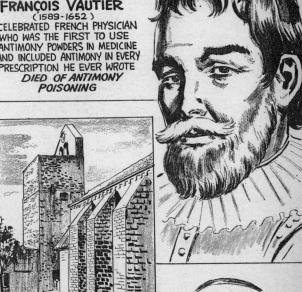

## FRANÇOIS VAUTIER
(1589-1652)
CELEBRATED FRENCH PHYSICIAN
WHO WAS THE FIRST TO USE
ANTIMONY POWDERS IN MEDICINE
AND INCLUDED ANTIMONY IN EVERY
PRESCRIPTION HE EVER WROTE
*DIED OF ANTIMONY
POISONING*

THE *CHURCH* of *VAUCLUSE* In France
NOW 1,400 YEARS OLD,
WAS BUILT IN THE 6th CENTURY
OUT OF THE DEBRIS FROM AN
ANCIENT TEMPLE--*WHICH HAD
BEEN IN RUINS FOR 500 YEARS*

## MARTIN M. LOMASNEY
(1859-1908) LEADER OF A BOSTON POLITICAL WARD,
ATE APPLESAUCE FOR BREAKFAST, LUNCH AND DINNER
*EVERY DAY OF HIS LIFE*

## THE FIRST TASMANIAN RAILWAY
A 5-MILE RAILROAD BUILT IN 1836 *HAD CARS PUSHED OVER WOODEN RAILS BY CONVICT LABOR* THE FARE WAS ONE SHILLING·

*A* **HOUSE** BUILT IN FRANKFURT-ON -THE-MAIN, GERMANY, *WITHOUT A GROUND FLOOR -- TO CARRY OUT A STRANGE WHIM OF ITS OWNER*

## NICOLAS VAUQUELIN
(1567-1649) THE FRENCH POET REFUSED TO TUTOR THE OLDEST SON OF KING HENRY IV of France UNTIL HE WAS PROMISED THAT WHEN HIS PUPIL BECAME KING HE WOULD NOT HAVE TO ADDRESS HIM AS "*YOUR MAJESTY*" -BUT COULD FAMILIARLY CALL THE MONARCH "*LOUIS XIII*"

**DRINKERS** IN LOWER SAXONY, GERMANY, DEMONSTRATE THEIR TECHNIQUE IN GULPING DOWN BEER, KÜMMEL AND VODKA FROM **3** GLASSES --*AT THE SAME TIME*

## GIROLAMO FRACASTORO

(1483-1553) of Verona, Italy, PRACTICED MEDICINE ALL HIS LIFE *WITHOUT EVER CHARGING A FEE--* HE WAS BORN WITH HIS LIPS SEALED AND SURGERY SAVED HIS LIFE--THEN LIGHTNING KILLED HIS MOTHER WHILE HE WAS BEING CARRIED IN HER ARMS AND HE *ESCAPED WITHOUT A SCRATCH*

*THE* **BLESSING** **OF MOHAMMED** IS BUILT INTO THE WALLS OF MOSQUES AND SCHOOLS IN MOROCCO IN A SPECIAL SQUARE WRITING STYLE WHICH CAN BE SPELLED OUT *IN BLACK AND WHITE BRICKS*

**THE** **PENDANT** **OF OFFICE** WORN BY MAORI CHIEFS of N. Zealand WAS AN EARRING MADE FROM THE DRIED HEAD OF A HUIA BIRD

LIZARD WITH **2** TAILS

## THE BANQUETS THAT ALWAYS ENDED WITHOUT A SINGLE DISH TO BE WASHED

**GODFREY MALBONE** of NEWPORT, R.I., WEALTHY SHIP OWNER, GAVE AN ANNUAL DINNER FOR HIS CAPTAINS AT THE FINISH OF WHICH HIS GUESTS WERE DIRECTED TO *SMASH EVERY PIECE OF CHINA USED DURING THE MEAL*

**INFANTS** IN THE TORTOISE TOTEM OF THE OSAGE INDIANS WERE GIVEN HAIRCUTS INDICATING *THE HEAD, PAWS AND TAIL OF A TORTOISE*

**CHARIOT WHEELS** CONSTRUCTED OF SECTIONS OF WOOD JOINED WITH COPPER NAILS, AND EXCAVATED AT KISH, IRAQ, IN 1928, *WERE USED 5,200 YEARS AGO*

**GIRLS** OF REMETE, CROATIA, ALWAYS PRESS THEIR LIGHT, FILMY GOWNS *WITH A STONE* WHILE THE MATERIAL IS WET

THE **EARLIEST GUILLOTINES** IN MEDIEVAL GERMANY USED AS THEIR BLADE A PIECE *OF DRIFTWOOD* — IF A VICTIM SURVIVED A SINGLE DROP OF THE BLADE HE WAS IMMEDIATELY FREED

THE **JAWBONE** OF EACH DECEASED KING OF THE BAGANDA TRIBE OF AFRICA IS REVERENTLY PRESERVED BY HIS SUCCESSOR IN THE BELIEF IT WILL ENABLE HIM TO *SPEAK WITH WISDOM*

THE **STRANGEST ACT OF GALLANTRY IN HISTORY** *Peter Sonnavater* SENTENCED TO BE HANGED FOR TREASON IN STOCKHOLM, SWEDEN, IN 1526, AS HIS LAST ACT *DRANK A TOAST TO THE HEALTH OF HIS EXECUTIONER*

**A NOOSE**
FOR YEARS WAS SENT BY THE CHIEF OF AN ISLAND IN NEW CALEDONIA TO THE CHIEF OF ANOTHER ISLAND TO WHICH ONE OF HIS TRIBESMEN HAD FLED--
THE NOOSE WAS EVENTUALLY SENT BACK, WITH ITS KNOT TIGHT --ASSURANCE THAT THE FUGITIVE HAD BEEN STRANGLED

**THE FISH THAT STANDS ON ITS HEAD** ( Chilodus punctatus ) of So. America SWIMS IN A VERTICAL POSITION WITH ITS TAIL UP AND HEAD DOWN

**PIE CRUST ICE**
A NATURAL PHENOMENON IN THE ANTARCTIC-- IT CONSISTS OF CLEAR ICE, FORCED UP FROM THE DIRTY ICE AROUND IT BY THAWS, AND OFTEN JUTS UP TO A HEIGHT OF ONE FOOT AND MEASURES AS MUCH AS 10 FEET IN DIAMETER

**CHIEF IRON SHIRT** of the Comanche Indians of Texas ALWAYS FOUGHT IN A STEEL BREASTPLATE WHICH AN ANCESTOR HAD TAKEN FROM ONE OF CORONADO'S KNIGHTS IN THE 16th CENTURY --HE HAD CLAIMED A CHARMED LIFE --BUT HE WAS KILLED BY A TEXAS RANGER'S BULLET

THE **FIRST EGYPTIAN FLAG** COMPRISED A REPLICA OF *THE PHARAOH'S LIVER* THE EGYPTIANS BELIEVED IT WAS THE REPOSITORY OF ALL HIS WISDOM

**JOSEPH NICOLAS FORLENZE** (1769-1833) FRENCH PHYSICIAN, SERVED ON THE STAFF OF **118** HOSPITALS--*EVERY HOSPITAL IN FRANCE IN HIS DAY*-- AND **210** *CHARITABLE INSTITUTIONS*

**AN OLD LINDEN TREE** IN SÜDERBASTEDT, GERMANY, USED FOR CENTURIES AS A PILLORY, STILL HAS ATTACHED TO IT *THE ANCIENT CHAIN WHICH SECURED TRANSGRESSORS*

**THE BASIN** OF THE ANCIENT FOUNTAIN IN THE COURTYARD OF THE MAFFEI PALACE, IN ROME, ITALY, *IS AN OLD SARCOPHAGUS*

THE **OREGON RUFFED GROUSE** BY STRIKING ITS WINGS AGAINST ITS CHEST *PRODUCES A DRUMLIKE SOUND THAT CAN BE HEARD A GREAT DISTANCE AWAY*

## BLAISE PASCAL
### (1623-1662)

THE FRENCH MATHEMATICAL GENIUS "INVENTED" GEOMETRY *WITHOUT HELP FROM A TEACHER OR TEXTBOOKS OF ANY KIND*

AT THE AGE OF **12**, PLAYING ON THE TILED FLOOR OF HIS HOME, HE WORKED OUT THE PRINCIPLES OF EUCLIDIAN GEOMETRY--REACHING THE **32nd** PROPOSITION OF EUCLID

THE **FEMALE CERATIOID ANGLER** *IS 50 TIMES AS LARGE AS THE MALE* 2 MALES REMAIN FIRMLY ATTACHED TO THE FEMALE'S SIDE THROUGHOUT THEIR LIFETIME

### THE CHURCH OF ST. KATHARINE

In Kleinkirchheim, Austria, WAS BUILT OVER A SPRING OF WARM MINERAL WATER, AND *THE ILL BATHE IN ITS WATERS WHILE PRAYING FOR A SPEEDY RECOVERY*

## THE SINGING RIVER

THE PASCAGOULA RIVER in MISSISSIPPI *MYSTERIOUSLY HUMS EVERY NIGHT AT TWILIGHT*

## KELLY HAUSER

of Shreveport, La., ATTENDED ELEMENTARY SCHOOL, JUNIOR HIGH AND HIGH SCHOOL WITHOUT A SINGLE DAY'S ABSENCE --*A PERFECT RECORD FOR 12 YEARS*

## VON der EMDEN

A GLASS MANUFACTURER IN FRANKFURT, GERMANY, DURING THE FINAL 22 YEARS OF HIS LIFE *DRANK 30 LARGE GLASSES OF CIDER EVERY DAY*

BEHOLD I COME AS A THIEF BLESSED IS HE WHO WATCHETH AND KEEPETH HIS GARMENTS

STRANGE EPITAPH OF BLUAJAH GILBERT In So. Salem, N.Y., Cemetery

## PHILIPPE de VENDÔME
### (1655-1727)
GRAND PRIOR OF FRANCE AND
A DISTINGUISHED WARRIOR
*BATHED ONLY 4 TIMES
IN HIS ENTIRE LIFETIME
OF 72 YEARS*

**SMALL MOUNTAIN CAVES**
IN GARIAN, LIBYA, ARE THE HOMES
*OF 20,000 PEOPLE*

## THE **HEAD** OF GARIBALDI
NATURAL ROCK FORMATION
IN THE LIBYAN DESERT,
IN FEZZAN, Libya

SCHLEHAN'S HOUSELEEK IS PROPAGATED *BY ITS ROSETTES* CLUSTERS OF PETALS, BLOWN TO THE GROUND, TAKE ROOT AND DEVELOP NEW FLOWERS THE FOLLOWING YEAR

## LUIS de VARGAS
### (1502-1568)
A NOTED PAINTER OF SEVILLE, SPAIN, ALWAYS WORKED AT HIS EASEL IN A SHROUD *--AND RESTED 4 HOURS EACH DAY IN A COFFIN*

T<sup>HE</sup> **DON BOSCO CHURCH** IN GRAZ, AUSTRIA, WAS ORIGINALLY USED FOR 200 YEARS *AS A POWDER MAGAZINE*

THE **PACIFIC NIGHTHAWK** IS HATCHED WITH LEGS ON WHICH IT CAN RUN SWIFTLY *--BUT ITS LEGS WITHER AWAY AS SOON AS IT BEGINS TO FLY*

**WIDOWS** VISITING THE TOMB OF A DECEASED HUSBAND IN CALABRIA, ITALY, ARE EXPECTED TO PUNCTURE A FINGER *TO LEAVE A FEW DROPS OF BLOOD ON THE GRAVE*

**XYLOPHONES** USED BY MUSICIANS ON THE CANARY ISLANDS STILL HAVE KEYS MADE FROM *BONES*

**DR. Thomas Cochrane** (1873-1953) ENGLISH MISSIONARY TO CHINA, WAS NOT PERMITTED TO OPERATE ON A LADY OF THE IMPERIAL COURT UNTIL HE HAD BECOME HER BROTHER-IN-LAW --*BY A MARRIAGE CEREMONY TO A FICTITIOUS SISTER OF THE PATIENT*

**CAN YOU REARRANGE THESE 12 COINS TO FORM 7 ROWS OF 4 COINS EACH?**

**HOW TO REARRANGE THESE 12 COINS...** --*TO FORM 7 ROWS OF 4 COINS EACH*

1---
2---
3---
4---
5   6   7

94

THE **RAIN** FOUNTAIN
IN THE GARDENS OF THE QUIRINALE
PALACE, IN ROME, ITALY,
HAS A CASCADE OF WATER
*THAT LOOKS LIKE A HEAVY
DOWNPOUR OF RAIN*

A STATUE of **ST. GENGULPH**
in Abbeville, France,
IS VISITED BY NEWLYWEDS
AS A PRECAUTION AGAINST
MARITAL DISCORD -- *BECAUSE
ST. GENGULPH IS CONSIDERED
THE PATRON SAINT OF
DECEIVED HUSBANDS*

NICCOLO TRIBOLO (1500-1565)
THE CELEBRATED ITALIAN SCULPTOR
*ALWAYS SLEPT WITH ONE EYE OPEN*

**1,000**
IN CHINESE
SYMBOLS IS
SIMPLER THAN
THE SYMBOL
*FOR ZERO*

千 零

LAKE HEMMELSDORF HAS A BED 145 FEET BELOW SEA LEVEL —THE LOWEST POINT IN ALL GERMANY

THE **CANDLE TREES** SONORA DESERT, MEXICO

TREES FOUND ONLY IN AN AREA OF 200 SQUARE MILES HAVE A BASE ONLY 18 INCHES IN DIAMETER AND NO LIMBS— YET THEY REACH A HEIGHT OF 50 FEET

AMALIE RENNER PEDDLED TRUMPETS, RULERS AND DOLLS IN A BEER CELLAR IN BRESLAU, GERMANY, FOR 60 YEARS— SHE NEVER WORKED ANY-WHERE ELSE

**THE CASTLE OF LUDWIGSTEIN**
A RUINED EDIFICE NEAR BAD SOODEN, GERMANY, WHICH WAS CONSTRUCTED IN 1415, IS PRESERVED AS *A MEMORIAL TO GERMAN SOLDIERS KILLED IN WORLD WAR I*

THE **MAN WHO WHIPPED 15,000 SOLDIERS** -- IN HIS OWN ARMY! APPIUS CLAUDIUS, COMMANDER IN 471 B.C. OF THE ROMAN ARMY, AS PUNISHMENT FOR ITS DEFEAT BY TROOPS OF THE VOLSCIANS, ORDERED 25 LASHES FOR EVERY PRIVATE IN HIS COMMAND -AND *50 LASHES FOR EVERY OFFICER*

THE **PALM OF PLENTY**
THE CARNAUBA PALM, of Brazil, PROVIDES *LUMBER* FOR HOMES, *FRUIT* USED AS FODDER, *THATCHING* FOR ROOFS, *GRAIN* FOR THE NATIVES' COFFEE, AND *WAX* USED TO MAKE PHONOGRAPH RECORDS

## TEX TYRRELL
WON A "TALL TALE" CONTEST IN ALICE SPRINGS, AUSTRALIA, BY TELLING INCREDIBLE STORIES *CONTINUOUSLY FOR 8 HOURS*

**THE BASEBALL FISH OF JOHORE** —Malaysia— BETTA BREDERI, A BREED OF FIGHTING FISH, PLAY BALL WITH THEIR EGGS, THE MALE AND FEMALE AERATING THEM BY *TOSSING THEM BACK AND FORTH*

**THE IMPERIAL BANQUETS** AT WHICH THE GUESTS LIFTED EVERYTHING IN SIGHT! EMPEROR LUCIUS VERUS, WHO RULED ROME FROM 161 TO 169, GAVE SUMPTUOUS BANQUETS FROM WHICH HIS GUESTS WERE PERMITTED TO TAKE HOME ALL THE PRECIOUS DISHES AND EATING IMPLEMENTS --AS WELL AS THE TRAINED SLAVES WHO HAD SERVED THEM

THE **LION'S HEAD**
Newport, Rhode Island,
NATURAL LAND FORMATION

**JAMES A. CARR**
A TEXAS RANGER
FIGHTING A BAND OF COMANCHE
INDIANS IN 1851, REMAINED ON
HIS FEET FOR HOURS WITH
*4 ARROWS IN HIS BODY*

THE **TRANSIENT CHURCH** in Jamestown, R.I.
IT WAS DESIGNED BY THE REV. CHARLES E. PRESTON IN 1899, SO IT
*COULD BE MOVED FROM PLACE TO PLACE BY 14 YOKE OF OXEN*

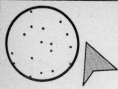

CAN YOU PLACE THE
SHADED ARROWHEAD
SO THAT ITS THREE
POINTS AND THE TIP
OF THE INNER ANGLE
EACH TOUCH ONE
OF THE LITTLE
HOLES IN THE
CIRCLE?

Solution

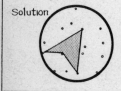

**EBENEZER PORTER MASON** (1819-1840)
THE CELEBRATED AMERICAN ASTRONOMER
COULD READ THE BIBLE FROM COVER TO COVER
*AT THE AGE OF 4*

**FIGHTS TO THE DEATH**
WERE STAGED IN OLD CALIFORNIA
*BETWEEN BULLS AND GRIZZLY BEARS*

**PRINCE RAINIER** of Monaco IS ALSO DUKE of VALENTINOIS MARQUIS of BAUX COUNT of CALARDEZ BARON of BUIS SIRE of MATIGNON LORD of SAINT-RÉMY COUNT of TORRIGNI BARON of RAMBYE BARON of LUTHUMIERE DUKE of MAZARIN BARON of ALTKIRCH PRINCE of CHATEAU-PORCIER MARQUIS of CHILLY BARON of MASSY AND MARQUIS of GUISCARD

THE **EMSCHER RIVER** A MAJOR TRANSPORTATION WATERWAY IN THE GERMAN RUHR *ORIGINATES IN THE CELLAR OF A FARMHOUSE IN HOLZWICKEDE*

THE **GREAT BREAD OVENS** IN RURAL CALABRIA, ITALY, BUILT OUTDOORS WITH HUGE BLOCKS OF STONE, HAVE NO MORTAR -- *YET HAVE BEEN USED FOR CENTURIES*

### THE **VIRGINIA HOUSE**
in Richmond, Va.,
WAS BUILT WITH MATERIAL
FROM THE PRIORY OF ST.
SUPULCHRE, WARWICK, ENGLAND,
*WHICH WAS CONSTRUCTED BY
THE FIRST EARL OF WARWICK
IN THE 11th CENTURY—*
ITS RIGHT WING, MOREOVER,
IS A REPLICA OF SULGRAVE
MANOR, THE ANCESTRAL
HOME OF THE FAMILY OF
GEORGE WASHINGTON

**DUKE HENRY** of Ratisbon, Germany,
WAS THE FIRST MAN
IN MODERN TIMES
TO USE A MENU—
AT A BANQUET IN 1489 HIS
CHEF PREPARED A LIST OF
DISHES TO BE SERVED SO *THE
DUKE WOULD NOT OVEREAT
ON THE FIRST COURSES*

**THE HOUSE OF THE SWAN**
in Rapperswil, Switzerland,
AS A MEMORIAL TO THE BRAVERY
OF ITS INHABITANTS DURING A
SIEGE IN 1656, STILL PRESERVES
IN ITS WALLS **3 STONE
CANNONBALLS**

GABRIEL SIONITE (1577-1648) A PROFESSOR OF ARABIC AT THE COLLEGE OF FRANCE, IN PARIS, LECTURED EVERY DAY FOR 12 YEARS --YET HE NEVER HAD A SINGLE STUDENT

A BEAUTIFUL STALACTITE CURTAIN IS DRAPED OVER THE ENTRANCE TO THE CAVE OF DARGILAN, NEAR MEYRUEIS, FRANCE

THE DANDY

Colonel WILLIAM ALDRIDGE FORT A PIONEER TEXAN, WEARING WHITE LINEN CLOTHING, RODE FROM LEIGHTON, ALABAMA, TO WACO, TEXAS -- A DISTANCE OF 900 MILES -- FORDED THE MUDDY TEHUACANA CREEK --AND THEN COLLECTED A BET HE HAD MADE THAT HIS GARB WOULD REMAIN IMMACULATE

**JOHN CREASEY** OF BODENHAM, ENGLAND, WHO HAS HAD **549** MYSTERY NOVELS PUBLISHED UNDER 25 NAMES *RECEIVED 743 REJECTION SLIPS BEFORE HIS FIRST BOOK WAS ACCEPTED*

THE **BELFRY** OF THE CHURCH OF NOTRE DAME de LIESSE, IN ANNECY, FRANCE, WHICH WAS BUILT IN THE 12th CENTURY *LEANS ONE FOOT, EIGHT INCHES OFF CENTER*

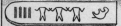

THE **EPITAPH** ON THIS OJIBWAY INDIAN TOMBSTONE READS, IN PICTURE LANGUAGE: Hear lies Chief Bear Mourned by his relatives and friends. A hero who slew four of his enemies -LAKE SUPERIOR REGION-

**CÉSAR** de **VENDÔME** (1594-1665) WAS GOVERNOR OF THE ENTIRE PROVINCE OF BRITTANY, FRANCE, *AT THE AGE OF 4*

**THE COMBS**
USED BY NATIVES OF MADAGASCAR ON THEIR FIBER MATS *ARE MADE FROM THE JAWBONES OF OXEN*

A **3-STORY APARTMENT HOUSE** in Graz, Austria, *WAS FOR 300 YEARS THE CHURCH OF ST. LEONHARD* --IN WHICH DIVINE SERVICES WERE HELD IN THE 15th, 16th AND 17th CENTURIES

## THE JEST THAT SAVED A JESTER!

TRIBOULET, COURT JESTER OF BOTH KING LOUIS XII AND FRANCIS I, UNDER SENTENCE OF DEATH FOR HAVING INSULTED A LADY OF THE COURT, WAS GIVEN PERMISSION TO CHOOSE HOW HE WOULD DIE— HE REPLIED: *"Of old age"* AND *THAT JEST SPARED HIS LIFE*

THE **SMALLEST RAILWAY IN THE WORLD** A STEAM LOCOMOTIVE THAT PULLS A TRAIN FROM HYTHE TO DYMCHURCH, ENGLAND, *OVER TRACKS ONLY ONE FOOT WIDE*

**THE MATHEMATICAL FORMULA** FOR CALCULATING THE AREA OF A CIRCLE WAS FOUND IN A BOOK WRITTEN BY A ROYAL EGYPTIAN SCRIBE NAMED AHMES MORE THAN **3,600** YEARS AGO *THE BOOK IS THE OLDEST KNOWN VOLUME ON MATHEMATICS--AND ITS FORMULA WOULD HAVE FLUNKED A MODERN MATH STUDENT*

**THE CAPS** WORN BY THE DAMARA WOMEN OF SOUTHWEST AFRICA ARE STYLED AFTER THE *HEADGEAR OF MINERVA, THE GREEK GODDESS OF WISDOM* THEY OFTEN STUFF ITS UPPER SECTION WITH HAIR FROM THE TAIL OF A COW

**THE STUPID SKUA** AN ANTARCTIC GULL WHEN A ROCK IS HURLED AT IT *WILL ALWAYS FLY DIRECTLY AT THE MISSILE--INVARIABLY BEING STUNNED BY IT*

**MOHAMMEDAN TOMBSTONES** IN LIBYA, BEAR NEITHER EPITAPHS NOR ORNAMENTS --BUT THE PROMINENCE AND WEALTH OF THE DECEASED IS INDICATED *BY THE NUMBER OF STEPS ON THE TOMB'S PEDESTAL*

WHILE ON EARTH
MY KNEE WAS LAME
I HAD TO NURSE
AND HEED IT
BUT NOW I'VE GONE
TO A BETTER PLACE
WHERE I DO NOT
EVEN NEED IT

*EPITAPH* IN PLEASANT GROVE
CEMETERY, ITHACA, N.Y.

**CAVE PEARLS**
MILLIONS OF ROUND
FORMATIONS COVER
THE CAVERN OF
COUSOUNNE, NEAR
TROUCHIOL, FRANCE
*--CREATED OF THE SAME
MATERIAL AS ORIENTAL PEARLS*

**THE FIRST BAR**
A MARBLE COUNTER WITH CIRCULAR
RECESSES IN WHICH DRINKS
WERE KEPT WARM WAS FOUND
*IN THE BURIED CITY OF POMPEII,
ITALY, WHICH WAS DESTROYED
BY VESUVIUS IN 79 A.D.*

**JOHN DONNE**
( 1573-1631 )
DAYS BEFORE HIS DEATH
DONNED A SHROUD, PREACHED
HIS OWN FUNERAL SERMON,
AND POSED WITH CLOSED EYES FOR
*THE STATUE ON HIS GRAVE*

THE **ARROW POISON
BEETLE** of the
KALAHARI DESERT,
IN AFRICA,
IS SO NAMED
BECAUSE ITS GRUB
*PROVIDES THE
DEADLY POISON
NATIVES USE ON
THEIR ARROWS*

THE **SKULL** OF AUSTRIAN COMPOSER HAYDN, WHO DIED in 1809, *WAS STOLEN FROM HIS GRAVE A FEW DAYS AFTER HIS BURIAL AND IS NOW PRESERVED IN THE MUSICAL SOCIETY OF VIENNA* ANOTHER MAN'S SKULL WAS MISTAKENLY SEIZED BY AUTHORITIES IN 1820 AND RESTS WITH HAYDN'S REMAINS IN HIS TOMB IN EISENSTADT

THE **STRANGE SIGNATURE** USED BY **CHRISTOPHER COLUMBUS** FOR THE FIRST TIME ON OCT. 12, 1492, WAS NOT DECIPHERED UNTIL **443 YEARS LATER** (1935)

IT MEANS: **LORD** (*HIS TITLE AS ADMIRAL*)
**HIS EXALTED LORDSHIP** (*HIS TITLE AS VICEROY*)
**EXCELLENT, MAGNIFICENT AND ILLUSTRIOUS** (*HIS TITLES AS GOVERNOR OF THE NEW WORLD*)
**CHRISTOPHER**

A **CURRENCY** of New Caledonia CONSISTING OF FILED TIPS OF SHELLS THREADED ON A STRING —*A YARD OF THIS MONEY WOULD PURCHASE A NEW WIFE*

THE **AMERICAN CHAMELEON**, WHEN PURSUED, CAN PAINLESSLY SEVER ITS TAIL WHICH WRIGGLES ABOUT ON THE GROUND-- *DISTRACTING THE PREDATOR*

THE **STRANGE SHADOW OF THE SIERRA NEVADA**
Venezuela
EVERY MOUNTAIN CLIMBER IN THE EARLY-MORNING HOURS CASTS UPON THE ADJACENT CLOUDS *A SHADOW 100 FEET HIGH*

**EDWARD CHARRIER** of Groves, Texas, WAS BORN ON *MONDAY, OCTOBER 14,* 1907
HIS SON RICHARD WAS BORN ON *MONDAY, OCTOBER 14,* 1940
HIS GRANDSON, JERRY, WAS BORN ON *MONDAY, OCTOBER 14, 1963*
AND EACH WAS THE FIRST-BORN SON IN HIS FAMILY

THE **FIRST BRITISH CURRENCY** CONSISTED OF IRON BARS *EACH 2 FEET LONG AND WEIGHING ABOUT A POUND*

### KLAUS FLÜGGE

OFFICIAL EXECUTIONER OF HAMBURG, GERMANY, ORDERED TO CARRY OUT A SENTENCE OF DEATH ON THE ENTIRE CREW OF A PIRATE SHIP, ARRANGED THE CONDEMNED MEN IN GROUPS--*AND LOPPED OFF 6 HEADS WITH A SINGLE SWING OF HIS SWORD*

THE **ATTIC WINDOWS** OF THE CHAPEL OF THE INVALIDS, IN PARIS, FRANCE, ACTUALLY ARE **COATS** *OF ARMOR WHICH ADMIT DAYLIGHT THROUGH THE OPENINGS IN THEIR VISOR AND CHEST*

A **TOWER**, EXHIBITED IN OSAKA, JAPAN, *CREATED OUT OF 5,000,000 POSTCARDS*-- THEY WERE PART OF 93,000,000 CARDS MAILED IN A CONTEST TO SELECT THE **8** MOST BEAUTIFUL SIGHTS IN JAPAN

**DR. THEOPHILE de LAËNNEC** (1781-1826) A FRENCH PHYSICIAN, INVENTED THE STETHOSCOPE *TO SPARE THE FEELINGS OF A MODEST FEMALE PATIENT*— TO HEAR HER HEARTBEAT *HE ROLLED A SHEET OF PAPER INTO A CONE*

THE **REV. SAMUEL EARNSHAW** (1805-1888) BECAME A TEACHER AT THE CARVER STREET NATIONAL SCHOOL, IN SHEFFIELD, ENGLAND, IN 1813, AT *THE AGE OF 8*

THE **STATUE OF A BEAR** FOUND IN A CAVE AT MONTESPAN, FRANCE, WAS CREATED IN CLAY 15,000 YEARS AGO --*THE ARTIST USED THE ACTUAL HEAD OF A BEAR, WHICH LEFT ITS OUTLINE ON THE WALL WHEN IT DECOMPOSED*

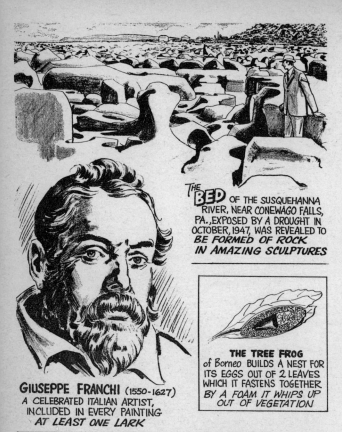

THE **BED** OF THE SUSQUEHANNA RIVER, NEAR CONEWAGO FALLS, PA., EXPOSED BY A DROUGHT IN OCTOBER, 1947, WAS REVEALED TO *BE FORMED OF ROCK IN AMAZING SCULPTURES*

**THE TREE FROG** of Borneo BUILDS A NEST FOR ITS EGGS OUT OF 2 LEAVES WHICH IT FASTENS TOGETHER *BY A FOAM IT WHIPS UP OUT OF VEGETATION*

**GIUSEPPE FRANCHI** (1550-1627) A CELEBRATED ITALIAN ARTIST, INCLUDED IN EVERY PAINTING *AT LEAST ONE LARK*

**ARZATE MOUNT** IN THE CHISOS RANGE OF TEXAS IS SHAPED LIKE THE PROFILE OF CHIEF ARZATE OF THE APACHES *--WHO ONCE HID IN THESE MOUNTAINS*

**A STABLE** in Ukuali, Somaliland, MADE BY MERELY PILING HUGE STONES WITHOUT MORTAR OF ANY KIND

THE **SYMBOL** OF **AUTHORITY** in Kano, Nigeria, WORN ONLY BY THE EMIR AND HIS FAMILY —**FANCY SLIPPERS** ADORNED WITH **OSTRICH FEATHERS**—

*THE MONARCH ALSO CARRIES 2 SPEARS TO COMMEMORATE TWIN BROTHERS WHO RULED TOGETHER IN ANCIENT TIMES*

THE **CALIFORNIAN BLIND GOBY** LIVES IN CREVICES IN ROCKS ON *THE SHORE*

WILL THE REAL ONE PLEASE STEP FORWARD?

**SERIAL NO. 04 028 121** WAS ISSUED BY THE U.S. ARMY **TO 2 MEN** —**MAJOR RICHARD T. SCHOFIELD** AND FIRST LIEUT. **RICHARD T. SCHOFIELD, JR.** THEY ARE NOT RELATED

*The* **GREEN MAN ENTERTAINMENT**

THE **WORD "ENTERTAINMENT"** ON INN SIGNS IN EARLY AMERICA MEANT ONLY *FOOD AND LODGING*

**THE FIRST ROCK SALT MINE IN AMERICA** ON AVERY ISLAND, LA., WHICH WAS DISCOVERED IN 1862, *IS STILL IN OPERATION-* THE BOTTOM OF ITS BED OF SOLID SALT STILL HAS NOT BEEN REACHED ALTHOUGH HOLES HAVE BEEN DRILLED *TO A DEPTH OF 2,200 FEET*

**THE REV. WILLIAM GILBERT LUCAS**
(1874-1947)
A PREACHER IN OKLAHOMA AND ALABAMA FOR 47 YEARS, INSISTED HE WAS OVER-PAID IN HIS FIRST YEAR WHEN HE WAS GIVEN AS HIS ANNUAL SALARY A *50¢ SHIRT AND A HANDFUL OF TOBACCO*
HE BUILT **21** CHURCHES AND FOUNDED **50** SUNDAY SCHOOLS

**THE SPOONS** USED BY BETSIMISARAKA TRIBESMEN OF MADAGASCAR ARE COMPLETELY DISPOSABLE BECAUSE THEY ARE MADE OF ARTFULLY FOLDED LEAVES

**A HEIFER** WHICH ESCAPED FROM ITS OWNER'S FARM IN PATAGONIA SWAM TO AN UNINHABITED ISLAND IN THE BLACK RIVER AND *BECAME THE LEADER OF A HERD OF WILD PIGS*

## SCOTTISH HIGHLANDERS

PRIOR TO 1700 WORE TARTAN KILTS MADE IN ONE PIECE, AND TO DON THE GARMENT THE HIGHLANDER HAD TO SPREAD THE CLOTH ON THE GROUND *AND LIE ON IT ON HIS BACK*

**FLUTES**
FOUND IN A PREHISTORIC CAVE ON THE ISLAND OF Bornholm, Denmark, *WERE MADE 6,000 YEARS AGO FROM HUMAN BONES*

### THE **HOLY WATER BASIN**
in the Church of St. Sulpice, in Paris, France, CONSISTS OF 2 HUGE SEA SHELLS

*ORIGINALLY GIVEN TO KING FRANCIS I BY THE CITY OF VENICE OVER 400 YEARS AGO*

THE **MEMORIAL** TO A CHIEF OF THE BETSILEO TRIBE OF MADAGASCAR WAS ALWAYS A HIGH TOWER, TOPPED BY ANIMAL HORNS FROM WHICH WAS HUNG A HUGE SPOON--*AS A REMINDER OF THE CHIEF'S GRACIOUS HOSPITALITY*

THE **MOUNTAIN GOAT**
IS NOT A GOAT—
*IT IS AKIN TO
THE ANTELOPE*

**JOHANN MICHAEL WIDMANN**
SERVED AS THE HANGMAN
IN NÜRNBERG, GERMANY,
*FOR 70 YEARS*

THE **AMAZING MAZE OF BUKURU**
Northern Nigeria, Africa—
THE ONLY PATH PERMITTING
ENTRANCE TO THE VILLAGE
IS A TWISTING TUNNEL LINED
WITH SPIKED CACTUS TREES,
AND UNLESS ACCOMPANIED
BY A GUIDE A STRANGER
*WOULD NEVER FIND HIS
WAY OUT OF THE COUNTLESS
BLIND ALLEYS*

**ABD el RAHMAN** (720-790)
Ruler of Tiaret, Algeria,
IN HIS LIFETIME OF **70 YEARS**
**NEVER ONCE TOUCHED MONEY**
*HE HANDLED IT ONLY BY MEANS OF A LONG FORKED STICK*

**SOPHONISBA** the Carthaginian princess who married King Masinissa, of Numidia, FEARFUL THAT THE ROMANS WOULD PERSUADE HER HUSBAND TO TURN AGAINST HER, ASKED HIM FOR ONLY ONE WEDDING GIFT -- *A CUP OF POISON* (203 B.C.)

**WATER BUCKETS** USED BY NATIVES OF Somaliland, Africa, *ARE MADE FROM THE STOMACH OF A CAMEL*

THE **STRANGE SENTINELS OF SUMATRA** Indonesia

**WATCHMEN** CARVED FROM WOOD *COMPLETE WITH A GUN FOR PROTECTION AND A BLANKET FOR WARMTH* GUARD THE GRAVES OF THE CHIEFS OF THE KARO BATAK TRIBE

117

THE **BAPTISMAL** FONT OF THE CHURCH OF WITTLAER, GERMANY, IS THE FACE OF THE 12th-CENTURY SCULPTOR WHO CARVED IT *--YET HIS NAME HAS LONG SINCE BEEN FORGOTTEN*

THE **JAPANESE ICHNEUMON FLY** HAS AN OVIPOSITOR *-THE EXTENSION IT USES TO DIG HOLES TO DEPOSIT ITS EGGS --9 TIMES AS LONG AS ITS BODY*

**THE STRANGEST RAILWAY ACCIDENT IN EUROPE**
THE ORIENT EXPRESS, TRAVELING AT A SPEED OF 43 MILES AN HOUR, CRASHED INTO THE CROWDED DINING ROOM OF THE STATION AT FRANKFURT ON THE MAIN, GERMANY, BREAKING A HOLE 33 FEET WIDE AND 40 FEET HIGH IN THE 5-FOOT-THICK WALL *--YET NO ONE WAS INJURED AND THE TRAIN ITSELF WAS NOT DAMAGED* – Dec. 6, 1901 -

THE **NEST** OF THE INDIAN RED ANT IS MADE FROM A SINGLE LARGE LEAF WHICH THE ANTS FOLD FROM TIP TO STEM BY FORMING THEMSELVES INTO A LIVING CHAIN

THE **BLACK MOUND TERMITE QUEEN** HAS 4 EYES *--YET SHE USES THEM FOR ONLY A FEW MOMENTS DURING HER ENTIRE LIFETIME* EXCEPT FOR A 50-YARD PRENUPTIAL FLIGHT, SHE SPENDS HER LIFE IN A PITCH-BLACK NEST

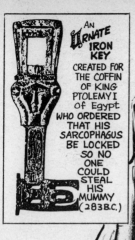

AN **O**RNATE **IRON KEY** CREATED FOR THE COFFIN OF KING PTOLEMY I OF EGYPT WHO ORDERED THAT HIS SARCOPHAGUS BE LOCKED SO NO ONE COULD STEAL HIS MUMMY (283 B.C.)

## MULEY ARCHID
[ 1631-1672 ]
IMPRISONED AND SENTENCED TO DEATH BY HIS OWN BROTHER, MOROCCAN EMPEROR MULEY MOHAMMED, WAS FREED BY THE HEROIC ACTION OF A LOYAL SLAVE--AND HIS FIRST ACT AFTER BEING LIBERATED *WAS TO KILL THE SLAVE--* HAVING SLAIN HIS LIBERATOR TO AVOID ANY POSSIBLE BETRAYAL, HE HID UNTIL HIS BROTHER'S DEATH, AND THEN RULED MOROCCO FOR 8 YEARS

**ZANY** COMES FROM SANNIO, THE *BUFFOON WHO STARRED IN COMIC PLAYS IN ANCIENT ROME*

A **FIG TREE** IN ROSCOFF, FRANCE, WHICH HAS FLOURISHED SINCE 1625 ALTHOUGH IT IS ONE OF THE MOST NORTHERN FIG TREES IN THE WORLD, NOW COVERS AN AREA OF 6,000 SQ. FEET

**J.E. ROBERTS** of WELLINGTON, TEXAS, WHILE A RAILROAD TELEGRAPHER IN HARROLD, TEXAS, IN 1934, TRAVELED **66** MILES A DAY TO AND FROM HIS HOME IN CHILLICOTHE · A TOTAL OF **24,090** MILES -- *ALWAYS BY HITCHHIKING*

THE **NORDERNEY LIGHTHOUSE**, GERMANY, 197 FEET HIGH— TO ENABLE IT TO WITHSTAND THE VIOLENT WINDS WAS BUILT SO THAT IT SWAYS AS MUCH AS *2 FEET OFF CENTER*

**THE GUAYACURÚS** A WARLIKE TRIBE OF PARAGUAY, PERISHED IN THE 18th CENTURY BECAUSE, IN AN EFFORT TO INCREASE THEIR MOBILITY, *THEY HAD ALWAYS KILLED OFF AT BIRTH ALL BUT ONE BABY IN EACH FAMILY*

**MOUNTAINS** THAT STRETCH FOR MILES IN THE RUB-AL-KHALI DESERT, IN SOUTHERN ARABIA, *CONSIST ENTIRELY OF ROCK SALT AND SOFT COAL*

THE **EXQUISITELY CARVED PULPIT** OF THE CHURCH IN VILLINGEN, GERMANY, WAS CREATED BY A *BLIND ARTIST*

AN **APACHE MEDICINE MAN** WAS PERMITTED TO **LOSE ONLY 6 PATIENTS TO DEATH** *IF A SEVENTH DIED HE WAS KILLED*

THE **NEST** OF THE WHITE-EARED HUMMINGBIRD IS PADDED WITH HAIR *WHICH IT STEALS FROM THE NESTS OF WASPS*

**TUCUNA INDIANS** OF BRAZIL'S AMAZON REGION, DURING THEIR FESTIVALS *BLOW BARK PIPES 20 FEET LONG*

**HOUSES** IN ALASSIO, ITALY, AS PROTECTION AGAINST EARTHQUAKES, ARE JOINED *BY ARCHES WHICH EXTEND ACROSS THE NARROW STREETS*

THE **MARAJAHY** a Brazilian fruit LOOKS LIKE GRAPES AND IS VERY SAVORY *-BUT ITS SKIN IS SO POISONOUS THAT THE LIPS BLISTER ON CONTACT*

**MURARI ADITYA** of Calcutta, India, LET HIS FINGERNAILS GROW TO A LENGTH OF **7 INCHES**

## THE MOST PERSISTENT SUITOR IN HISTORY

PONTHUS, A SPANISH PRINCE SHIPWRECKED ON THE COAST OF FRENCH BRITTANY IN THE 12th CENTURY, WON THE HAND OF A LOCAL PRINCESS NAMED SIDOINE, *ONLY AFTER DEFEATING 50 RIVALS IN KNIGHTLY COMBAT*

## WILLIAM CHART

OF MITCHAM, AUSTRALIA, SERVED AS PARISH CLERK FOR 44 YEARS -- HIS SON HELD THE OFFICE FOR 41 YEARS -- HIS GRANDSON WAS CLERK FOR 40 YEARS -- HIS GREAT-GRANDSON HAD THE JOB 29 YEARS -- HIS GREAT-GREAT-GRANDSON FOR 19 YEARS -- *FIVE GENERATIONS SERVING A TOTAL OF 173 YEARS*

## THE HEAVIEST FIGUREHEAD

THE KNIGHT SCULPTED AS FIGUREHEAD OF THE 5-MASTED BARK "KOBENHAVN" WAS MADE OF SOLID BRASS AND WEIGHED 12 TONS

123

## THE FIVE-FINGERED TREE
A LINDEN TREE GROWING IN ODDERADE, GERMANY, *HAS THE SHAPE OF A HUMAN HAND WITH THUMB AND FINGERS EXTENDED*

## CHURCH MUSIC
IN THE BALEARIC ISLANDS OF SPAIN
IS OFTEN PLAYED ON **THE BLADE OF A SWORD**
*THE MUSICAL SWORD IS TAPPED WITH THE FINGERS WHICH HAVE BEEN FITTED WITH METAL TIPS*

## A HARVARD STUDENT
IN A DEBATE ON THE ANNEXATION OF HAWAII IN 1902, STRESSED THAT PEARL HARBOR *COULD PLAY AN IMPORTANT ROLE IN THE U.S. NAVY!* 39 YEARS LATER PEARL HARBOR'S NAVY ROLE WAS FORCIBLY CALLED TO THE ATTENTION OF THAT STUDENT --*FRANKLIN D. ROOSEVELT*

## THE ROCKING HOUSE
A HOME in St. Pankraz, Tyrol, IS BUILT ON A GIANT ROCKING BOULDER --AND *TEETERS IN THE WIND*

## "JUMPING SAM" PATCH
( 1807- 1829 )
SAFELY LEAPED INTO NIAGARA FALLS FROM A PLATFORM 125 FEET ABOVE THE WATER --*BUT ONE MONTH LATER HE REPEATED THE FEAT AT GENESEE FALLS, N.Y. --AND WAS DROWNED*

## THE GLASSWORT
WHICH GROWS IN SALTY SEACOAST MARSHES PREPARES THE GROUND FOR OTHER PLANTS --*ITS ROOTS STABILIZING THE SOIL*

A WOODEN CONE
INSERTED BY ESKIMO HUNTERS IN WOUNDED ANIMALS BECAUSE THEY BELIEVE THAT *IT IS SINFUL TO ALLOW BLOOD TO FLOW ONTO THE GROUND*

## "LIGHTNING CONDUCTORS"
WERE INVENTED BY THE ZULUS OF AFRICA --*WHO NEVER HEARD OF BENJAMIN FRANKLIN OR THE NECESSITY OF GROUNDING THEM* THEY PLACED SHARP-POINTED IRON RODS ON THEIR HUTS TO PROTECT THEM FROM LIGHTNING AND EVIL SPIRITS

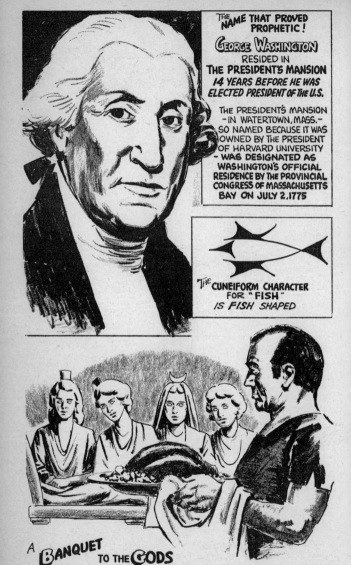

**THE NAME THAT PROVED PROPHETIC!**

**GEORGE WASHINGTON** RESIDED IN **THE PRESIDENT'S MANSION** *14 YEARS BEFORE HE WAS ELECTED PRESIDENT OF THE U.S.*

THE PRESIDENT'S MANSION – IN WATERTOWN, MASS. – SO NAMED BECAUSE IT WAS OWNED BY THE PRESIDENT OF HARVARD UNIVERSITY – WAS DESIGNATED AS WASHINGTON'S OFFICIAL RESIDENCE BY THE PROVINCIAL CONGRESS OF MASSACHUSETTS BAY ON JULY 2, 1775

**THE CUNEIFORM CHARACTER FOR "FISH"** *IS FISH SHAPED*

**A BANQUET TO THE GODS** WAS STAGED EACH NOV. 13th IN THE ROMAN EMPIRE WITH THE GUESTS OF HONOR AT THE LAVISH MEAL *THE STATUES OF 4 GODS*

**MORGAN'S HEAD**
*NATURAL STONE FORMATION OFF SWAN ISLAND, JAMAICA*

**THE PRISON** ON TAHU ATA, ONE OF THE MARQUESAS ISLANDS, IN THE SOUTH PACIFIC, *NEVER LOCKS ITS DOORS—*
INMATES, SOME SERVING LIFE SENTENCES FOR MURDER, ARE PERMITTED TO LEAVE AT ANY TIME OF THE DAY TO WORK AT VARIOUS JOBS ON THE ISLAND

**THE STONE "XYLOPHONE"**
**HONORÉ BAUDRE**, of Huvergue, France, MADE A MUSICAL INSTRUMENT USING VIBRATING FLINT STONES --COLLECTED *OVER A PERIOD OF 30 YEARS*

**THE JACKSNIPE**
SINGS ITS SONG OF LOVE IN FLIGHT BY USING AS ITS VOICE *THE VIBRATION OF ITS WINGS*

**MONTANA** WHEN ORIGINALLY SUGGESTED AS THE NAME OF A U.S. TERRITORY, WAS REJECTED BY SECRETARY OF STATE CHARLES SUMNER *WHO INSISTED THERE WAS NO SUCH WORD—* JOHN ASHLEY, CHAIRMAN OF THE COMMITTEE THAT RECOMMENDED THE NAME, HAD A RESEARCHER CHECK THE LIBRARY OF CONGRESS FOR WEEKS--*AND FINALLY FOUND A SINGLE USE OF THE WORD IN "5th OF NOVEMBER", A POEM BY MILTON*

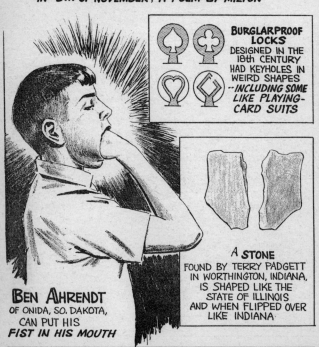

**BURGLARPROOF LOCKS** DESIGNED IN THE 18th CENTURY HAD KEYHOLES IN WEIRD SHAPES *--INCLUDING SOME LIKE PLAYING-CARD SUITS*

A **STONE** FOUND BY TERRY PADGETT IN WORTHINGTON, INDIANA, IS SHAPED LIKE THE STATE OF ILLINOIS AND WHEN FLIPPED OVER LIKE INDIANA

**BEN AHRENDT** OF ONIDA, SO. DAKOTA, CAN PUT HIS *FIST IN HIS MOUTH*

**PRIZED PETS** OF THE JAPANESE ARE SINGING FROGS —WHICH ARE KEPT CAGED SO THEIR OWNERS CAN ENJOY THEIR SWEET CHIRPING

**THE STAFF TREE** AN OLD TAMARIND TREE OUTSIDE THE TEMPLE OF DER ES-SURJANI, IN EGYPT'S NATRON DESERT, GREW FROM A STAFF PUSHED INTO THE GROUND AND THEN FORGOTTEN *BY ST. EPHRAIM*

**WIDOWS** IN ALBANIA STILL WEAR WHITE *AS THE COLOR OF MOURNING*

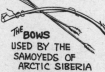

THE **BOWS** USED BY THE SAMOYEDS OF ARCTIC SIBERIA ARE ALWAYS HELD HORIZONTALLY AND ARE NEVER SHOT UNTIL THEY HAVE BEEN BENT *INSIDE OUT*

IN MEMORY OF MR. NATH PARKS AGE 19 WHO ON MARCH 21, 1794 BEING OUT HUNTING IN A DITCH WAS CASUALLY SHOT BY MRS. LUTHER FRINK

*Epitaph* IN ELMWOOD CEMETERY, HOLYOKE, MASS.

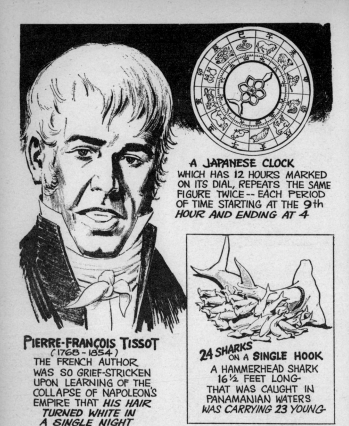

**A JAPANESE CLOCK**
WHICH HAS 12 HOURS MARKED
ON ITS DIAL, REPEATS THE SAME
FIGURE TWICE -- EACH PERIOD
OF TIME STARTING AT THE *9th
HOUR AND ENDING AT 4*

**PIERRE-FRANÇOIS TISSOT**
(1768 - 1854)
THE FRENCH AUTHOR
WAS SO GRIEF-STRICKEN
UPON LEARNING OF THE
COLLAPSE OF NAPOLEON'S
EMPIRE THAT *HIS HAIR
TURNED WHITE IN
A SINGLE NIGHT*

*24 SHARKS* ON A **SINGLE HOOK**
A HAMMERHEAD SHARK
16½ FEET LONG
THAT WAS CAUGHT IN
PANAMANIAN WATERS
WAS CARRYING 23 YOUNG

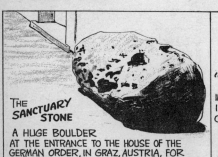

THE **SANCTUARY STONE**

A HUGE BOULDER
AT THE ENTRANCE TO THE HOUSE OF THE
GERMAN ORDER, IN GRAZ, AUSTRIA, FOR
CENTURIES OFFERED IMMUNITY FROM PUNISH-
MENT TO ANY FUGITIVE WHO RESTED A FOOT ON IT

**"GRACIOUS"**
IN CHINESE SCRIPT
IS EXPRESSED BY A
CHARACTER DEPICTING
2 WOMEN
*THE CHARACTER
DEPICTING THREE
WOMEN EXPRESSES
"INFIDELITY"*

130

THE **CHURCH** of **CELLA** di **VARSI**
IN ITALY
WAS BUILT AS A WAR MEMORIAL
*FROM THE DEBRIS OF
SCORES OF BOMBED CHURCHES*

DR. **DAVID S. MAYNARD**
( 1808-1873 ) OF SEATTLE,
WASHINGTON TERRITORY,
SERVED SIMULTANEOUSLY AS
*A PHYSICIAN, DRUGGIST,
SCHOOL SUPERINTENDENT,
STOREKEEPER, JUSTICE OF
THE PEACE, COURT CLERK,
NOTARY PUBLIC, INDIAN
AGENT, LUMBERMAN, REAL
ESTATE OPERATOR, FARMER,
TEAMSTER, BLACKSMITH,
U.S. COMMISSIONER,
ATTORNEY AND MINISTER*

**THE STREET OF LIFE AND DEATH**
IN Avila, Spain,
NAMED FOR A MEDALLION DEPICTING
A SMILING GIRL AND A SKULL
*IS A DEAD-END STREET*

**THE BLIND CRAYFISH**
WHICH LIVES IN CAVES
HAS LONG HAIRS ON ITS
CLAWS--*TO ENHANCE
ITS SENSE OF TOUCH*

**LETTER CARRIERS** in Denmark WHO HAVE TO CROSS SHALLOW RIVERS AND MARSHES, WALK ON STILTS -- *AND CARRY THEIR MAIL IN A WATERPROOF COMPARTMENT IN THE LEFT STILT*

**10 ENTIRE VILLAGES** IN THE SANGHA REGION of the African Sudan *ARE BUILT IN CAVES OR HALFWAY UP A STEEP CLIFF.* TO ASSURE A SUPPLY OF FOOD EVEN WHEN UNDER ATTACK, NATIVES HAVE BUILT GARDENS ON FLAT ROCKS *BY HAULING UP SOIL FROM THE VALLEY A BASKET AT A TIME*

**THE OLDEST HOTEL IN ALL GERMANY** THE GIANT, in Miltenberg, OPENED FOR BUSINESS AS A HOTEL IN **1590**

**A POLICEMAN'S BILLY** PATENTED IN ENGLAND IN 1887, COULD SEND A DISTRESS SIGNAL BY *CONVERTING IT INTO A ROMAN CANDLE*

THE **GREAT GRANITE CROSS OF ARRADON**, France, 30 FEET HIGH, DIFFERS FROM ALL OTHER CROSSES IN THAT THE FIGURE OF CHRIST ON IT *WAS CARVED FROM THE SAME BLOCK OF GRANITE AS THE CROSS ITSELF*

THE **REV. ALEXANDER JOHN FORSYTH** ( 1769- 1843 ) BRITISH INVENTOR OF THE PERCUSSION GUN LOCK WHICH REVOLUTIONIZED WARFARE, REFUSED TO SELL HIS INVENTION TO EMPEROR NAPOLEON I OF FRANCE FOR $100,000 — PATRIOTICALLY, HE GAVE HIS INVENTION TO THE BRITISH GOVERNMENT IN 1808 FOR $5,000, *BUT THE MONEY WAS NOT PAID UNTIL 35 YEARS LATER -- SIX MONTHS AFTER FORSYTH'S DEATH*

THE **HITCH-HIKING TREE** NATURAL FORMATION ON HIGHWAY 24, NEAR COLLINGWOOD, ONT.

THE **UNMERRY MONARCH** *KING MAXIMILIAN II* (1811-1864) of Bavaria IN HIS ENTIRE LIFETIME *NEVER SMILED*

133

**THE HOLE IN THE WALL**
AN INN IN COLCHESTER, ENGLAND,
WAS BUILT ON TOP OF THE
ANCIENT ROMAN WALL--*ABOVE
A GATE THROUGH WHICH
PASSED THE ROAD TO LONDON*

**JOSIAH BARTLETT**
(1729-1795) of New Hampshire
CAST THE FIRST VOTE FOR AMERICAN
INDEPENDENCE IN 1776--*BECAUSE
HE REPRESENTED THE MOST
EASTERLY PROVINCE IN THE COLONIES*
HE WAS CHIEF JUSTICE OF NEW
HAMPSHIRE--BUT HE WAS A
PHYSICIAN AND NOT A LAWYER

**MILLET CEREAL**
IS ALWAYS
SERVED BY THE
BAFUM TRIBE
of AFRICA
IN A WOODEN
DISH CARVED
IN THE FORM
OF A STATUE
OF THE COOK
WHO INVENTED
THE CEREAL

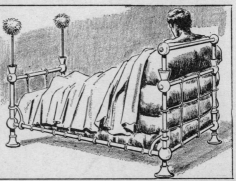

**EUROPEAN
ARISTOCRATS**
SLEPT IN THE
9TH CENTURY
AT AN ANGLE
OF 45 DEGREES
*WITH THEIR
HEAD AND
SHOULDERS
EXTENDING
BEYOND THE
EDGE OF
THE BED*

134

## THE TICKING ROCK OF LOUERES
### France
A PREHISTORIC MONUMENT WHICH FOR CENTURIES HAS MYSTERIOUSLY GIVEN OFF THE SOUND OF *A TICKING CLOCK*

### A STREETCAR
ON CHERRELYN ST., IN DENVER, Colo., UNTIL ITS DISCONTINUANCE IN 1910, WAS PULLED UPHILL BY A HORSE WHICH, ON THE RETURN TRIP DOWNHILL, *RODE AS A PASSENGER ON THE CAR'S BACK PLATFORM*

## THE MAN OF THE HOUR
COUNT d'ARTOIS (1757-1836) WHO LATER BECAME KING CHARLES X of France, WORE ON HIS CLOTHING AS BUTTONS GENUINE DIAMONDS -*EACH ENCASING A MINIATURE WATCH*

### THE EPITAPH
ON THE GRAVESTONE OF ROLAND GOOCK IN THE CEMETERY AT Gütersloh, Germany, *IS A REPLICA OF THE SEAL OF HIS PUBLISHING FIRM*

135

THE **GIANT** PETREL OF THE ANTARCTIC FOR A REASON THAT STILL MYSTIFIES SCIENCE, HAS A HOLE GOING THROUGH ITS BEAK *FROM SIDE TO SIDE*

**DR. JOHN MARSH** (1799-1856) WAS THE FIRST AMERICAN PHYSICIAN IN CALIFORNIA, THE FIRST SCHOOLMASTER IN MINNESOTA -- FOUND A GOLD MINE THAT MADE HIM WEALTHY, AND ALSO WAS A TRADER, AN INDIAN AGENT, A RANCHER, A MAIL CARRIER, AND A JUSTICE OF THE PEACE

THE **MOSQUE** IN THE CASTLE PARK of SCHWETZINGEN, GERMANY --WHERE SERVICES ARE HELD REGULARLY BY MOSLEM STUDENTS, WAS BUILT IN 1778 BY DUKE KARL THEODOR, ONLY AS *AN ARCHITECTURAL WHIM*

**DOLLS** USED BY THE SAMOYED CHILDREN OF ARCTIC SIBERIA, ARE MADE *FROM THE BEAKS OF GEESE*

THE **HEBREW LETTER "L"** ALSO IS THE NUMBER 30 -- *PLACING 2 DOTS OVER THE LETTER INCREASES ITS VALUE TO 30,000*

A **Z**URLA **PLAYER** OF MACEDONIA, YUGOSLAVIA, MUST BE ABLE TO STORE SUFFICIENT AIR IN HIS BULGING CHEEKS *TO PLAY AN ENTIRE DANCE NUMBER*

**GRAIN SHOVELS** USED BY EARLY AMERICAN FARMERS WERE CARVED FROM SOLID WOOD BECAUSE THEY BELIEVED THAT NOTHING MADE *OF IRON SHOULD TOUCH GRAIN*

**THE TEMPLE OF BARA KATRA** In Dacca, India, WAS CONSTRUCTED IN 1644 WITH 22 SHOPS AS PART OF THE EDIFICE *SO THEIR RENTAL COULD DEFRAY ITS MAINTENANCE COST-* THE FAÇADE BEARS THE INSCRIPTION: *"WHAT A BUILDING - IT PUTTETH HEAVEN TO SHAME - A COPY OF PARADISE - YOU MIGHT IT NAME"*

137

ZENZI TAU, A PEAK 12,500 FEET HIGH IN THE RUSSIAN CAUCASUS, IS NAMED AFTER ZENZI von FICKER, A GERMAN WOMAN ALPINIST, WHO WAS THE FIRST PERSON TO CLIMB IT--SHE WAS ALSO GIVEN OWNERSHIP OF THE MOUNTAIN IN 1903

SMOKE FROM A PIPE WITH ONE STEM AND 9 BOWLS IS BLOWN BY THE MEDICINE MAN OF THE MUKASA TRIBE OF AFRICA INTO THE FACE OF EACH PATIENT IN THE BELIEF *IT WILL CURE ANY AILMENT*

EVERY ENGLISHMAN BETWEEN THE AGES OF 15 AND 60 WAS REQUIRED IN THE 13th CENTURY *TO OWN A BOW AS LONG AS HIMSELF*

LOUIS COUNT d'ASSAS
[ 1820-1859 ] A FRENCH PLAYWRIGHT, LONG HECKLED FOR HIS SLOW WRITING, PLEDGED THAT HE WOULD CREATE A 5-ACT PLAY *WITHOUT PAUSING FOR SLEEP, FOOD OR DRINK—* HE COMPLETED IT IN 8 DAYS-- AND DIED AT HIS DESK, HIS WRITING QUILL SO TIGHTLY GRIPPED THAT HE WAS *BURIED WITH IT STILL BETWEEN HIS FINGERS*

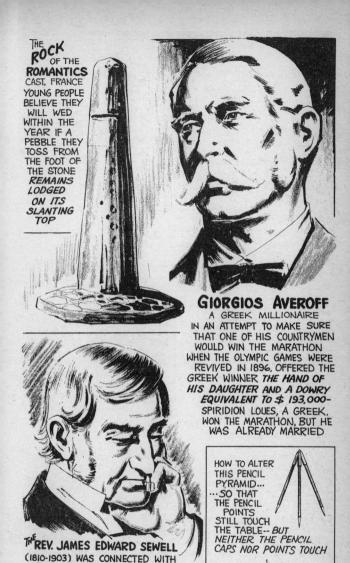

**THE ROCK OF THE ROMANTICS** CAST, FRANCE YOUNG PEOPLE BELIEVE THEY WILL WED WITHIN THE YEAR IF A PEBBLE THEY TOSS FROM THE FOOT OF THE STONE *REMAINS LODGED ON ITS SLANTING TOP*

**GIORGIOS AVEROFF** A GREEK MILLIONAIRE IN AN ATTEMPT TO MAKE SURE THAT ONE OF HIS COUNTRYMEN WOULD WIN THE MARATHON WHEN THE OLYMPIC GAMES WERE REVIVED IN 1896, OFFERED THE GREEK WINNER *THE HAND OF HIS DAUGHTER AND A DOWRY EQUIVALENT TO $193,000—* SPIRIDION LOUES, A GREEK, WON THE MARATHON, BUT HE WAS ALREADY MARRIED

**THE REV. JAMES EDWARD SEWELL** (1810-1903) WAS CONNECTED WITH NEW COLLEGE, OXFORD, ENGLAND, *CONTINUOUSLY FOR 77 YEARS—* HE STARTED AS A STUDENT AND AT HIS DEATH WAS ITS VICE-CHANCELLOR

HOW TO ALTER THIS PENCIL PYRAMID... ...SO THAT THE PENCIL POINTS STILL TOUCH THE TABLE-- BUT NEITHER THE PENCIL CAPS NOR POINTS TOUCH

THE **ROCKING** STONES of BUGANGADZI (Africa) GIANT BOULDERS BALANCED SO PRECARIOUSLY *THAT THE WIND ROCKS THEM BACK AND FORTH*

## WHITE STORKS

HATCH THEIR YOUNG BY THE MALE AND FEMALE **TAKING TURNS SITTING ON THE EGGS—** EACH CHANGEOVER IS MARKED BY AN ELABORATE CEREMONY OF WELCOME WITH CRIES OF JOY THAT CAN BE HEARD HALF A MILE AWAY

**MATTIA PRETI** (1613-1699) A NOTED ITALIAN PAINTER ENJOYED DRUMMING SO MUCH THAT WHILE PAINTING HE WOULD BEAT OUT RHYTHMS BY *DRUMMING AGAINST HIS TIGHTLY STRETCHED CANVAS WITH HIS BRUSH AND PALETTE*

THE **SEA-FIR** A PLANT-LIKE GROWTH IS CREATED BY TINY MARINE ANIMALS SO THEY CAN BUILD THEIR NESTS IN ITS BRANCHES

THE **RAFT SPIDER** BUILDS ITS NEST IN THE SHAPE OF A RAFT ON *WHICH IT SAILS IN SEARCH OF INSECTS*

**FLOWER POLES** ARE PLACED IN THE CHURCH OF ZEDERHAUS, AUSTRIA, BY NATIVES AS AN ACT OF REVERENCE --EACH POLE APPROXIMATELY **26** FEET LONG AND *DECORATED WITH MORE THAN* **25,000** *FLOWERS*

**ANTONIA** (35-66) DAUGHTER OF ROMAN EMPEROR CLAUDIUS, AFTER HAVING TWICE BEEN WIDOWED, *CHOSE DEATH IN PREFERENCE TO MARRYING EMPEROR NERO*

**MYODWIN** a town in Burma, BUILT IN **1386** ON MARSHY GROUND HAD **4** WOMEN BURIED ALIVE IN ITS FAR CORNERS — *IN THE BELIEF THIS WOULD KEEP THE VILLAGE ON AN EVEN KEEL*

141

THE **CHATEAU** de la **CAZE** in the Tarn region of France WAS CONSTRUCTED ENTIRELY FROM ROCKS EXCAVATED FOR ITS CELLAR AND MOAT

THE **COAT OF ARMS** OF THE BAKAMA TRIBE OF AFRICA

IS A DESIGN REPRE-SENTING THE KING'S CROWN AND TRADITIONAL MASK-- AND IS MADE WITH THE FUR OF THE COLOBUS MONKEY

**B**ERNARDO **G**AVINO (1813-1886) MEXICAN BULLFIGHTER FOUGHT HIS LAST BULL FOR A FEE OF $15 AT THE AGE OF 73

A **STREETCAR** IN BLACKPOOL, ENGLAND, AS A MEANS OF ATTRACTING MORE RIDERS, WAS MADE TO LOOK LIKE A WILD WEST TRAIN —HAVING BEEN COPIED FROM AMERICAN MOVIES

THE **TOMBSTONE** OF
BARTHOLOMÄUS VIATIS
(1538 - 1624)
A MERCHANT PRINCE
of Nürnberg, Germany,
IS ADORNED BY LIKENESSES
OF **15 CHILDREN**,
**31 GRANDCHILDREN** AND
**9 GREAT-GRANDCHILDREN**

THE **OSTRICH** ALWAYS LAYS ONE
OF ITS EGGS **OUTSIDE ITS NEST**-
NATIVES OF THE KALAHARI
DESERT, IN AFRICA, INSIST
THAT SEEING THE LONE EGG
BESIDE THE NEST HELPS TO
REMIND THE ABSENT-MINDED
MOTHER TO HATCH THE OTHERS

**CAVE DWELLINGS** in Sperlinga, Italy,
BUILT IN PREHISTORIC TIMES, ARE
PREFERRED BY NATIVES OVER
MODERN HOMES BECAUSE THEY
*ARE NATURALLY WARM IN WINTER
AND COOL IN SUMMER*

**CLAUDE NOISOT** ( 1787 - 1861)
A NAPOLEONIC SOLDIER,
PURSUING A WOLF HE WAS HUNTING,
RAN ALL THE WAY FROM FIXIN TO BRESSE,
FRANCE, A DISTANCE OF 37 MILES
*-- AT THE AGE OF 70*

**THE OLIVE TREES**
IN AN ANCIENT GROVE IN
CITTANOVA, ITALY, HAVE BEEN
SO BUFFETED BY HIGH WINDS
THAT *THEIR TRUNKS LOOK
LIKE CORKSCREWS*

THE **STRANGEST STATUE
IN THE WORLD**

**A HEAD OF HOMER**
CARVED IN 1889 BY THE
GERMAN SCULPTOR, SALA,
*BY CREATING 2 FULL-
SIZE STATUES OF THE 2
MYTHOLOGICAL CHARACTERS,
AMOR AND PSYCHE*
( Berlin )

THE **TREE** OF FEAR near Palma, Majorca,
WHICH FOR **400** YEARS HAS
BORNE FRUIT ONLY WHEN
*"FRIGHTENED" IN THE SPRING BY
DRUMS AND RATTLES*

PETITIONS
OF
Collar and Cuff
AND
SHIRT OPERATIVES

THE
LARGEST
PETITION
EVER
PRESENTED
TO
CONGRESS

*IT WEIGHED 580 POUNDS AND
CONTAINED 70,000 SIGNATURES*
1894

**LOUIS COUNT de FORBIN** (1777-1841)
WHO LATER BECAME A FAMOUS FRENCH
PAINTER AND ARCHEOLOGIST,
WAS MADE A KNIGHT OF MALTA
*ON THE DAY HE WAS BORN*

**THE BETSILEO BOUNCE**

*THE* CURE FOR ANY
ILLNESS AMONG
THE BETSILEO
TRIBESMEN OF
MADAGASCAR IS
PUTTING THE PATIENT
INTO A TRANCE--*AND
THEN ORDERING HIM
TO RISE FROM HIS
BED AND DANCE*--
AFTER A WEEK OF--
THIS TREATMENT THE
PATIENT IS USUALLY
CURED--OR DEAD

**SPIRIT TRAPS**
BASKETS ARE HUNG
IN HUTS IN CELEBES,
INDONESIA, IN THE BELIEF
THAT EVIL SPIRITS WILL
*BECOME ENTANGLED
IN THE FRINGE*

*THE* **PYRAMID OF MEROË** in Egypt
CONTAINING THE TOMB OF QUEEN AMANI, WAS DEMOLISHED LAYER
BY LAYER BY DR. GIUSEPPE FERLINI, AN ITALIAN PHYSICIAN, IN 1834,
*BECAUSE IN A CHILDHOOD DREAM HE HAD SEEN THE PYRAMID AS
THE HIDING PLACE OF A GREAT TREASURE*--FERLINI ACTUALLY FOUND
A TREASURE TROVE IN THE PYRAMID AND BECAME ENORMOUSLY WEALTHY

**THE TIMHADIT MILITARY POST** IN THE ATLAS MOUNTAINS OF MOROCCO IS LOCATED *INSIDE THE CRATER OF AN EXTINCT VOLCANO*

**THE VERMONT STATE FAIR** HELD IN WHITE RIVER JUNCTION, VT., *WAS PLAGUED BY RAIN THE ENTIRE WEEK ANNUALLY FOR 30 YEARS—* THE OPENING DATE WAS CHANGED REPEATEDLY IN AN ATTEMPT TO GET GOOD WEATHER--BUT IN 1928 THE FAIR WAS ABANDONED

**DE WITT CLINTON** (1769-1828) WHILE MAYOR OF NEW YORK CITY, AT DIFFERENT PERIODS WAS ALSO *A STATE SENATOR AND LIEUTENANT GOVERNOR OF THE STATE*

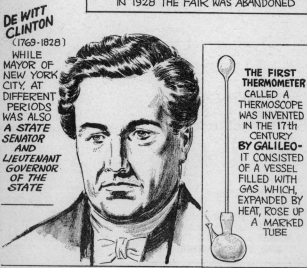

**THE FIRST THERMOMETER** CALLED A THERMOSCOPE WAS INVENTED IN THE 17th CENTURY **BY GALILEO—** IT CONSISTED OF A VESSEL FILLED WITH GAS WHICH, EXPANDED BY HEAT, ROSE UP A MARKED TUBE

**KING FREDERICK WILLIAM I** ( 1688-1740 ) of Prussia ATTEMPTING TO KISS A LADY OF THE COURT, MISS PANNEWITZ, WAS PUNCHED IN THE FACE BY HER SO HARD THAT *HE BLED FROM THE MOUTH AND NOSE-* THE MONARCH NEVER PUNISHED HER--AND *NEVER AGAIN ATTEMPTED TO KISS HER*

THE **BAKER ANTS** CRUSH AND POUND RICE INTO FLOUR AND ROLL IT INTO THE FORM OF ROUND CAKES --*WHICH THEY SET OUT TO BAKE IN THE SUN*

**ITALIAN PEASANTS** PRODUCE MUSIC FOR RURAL FOLK DANCES BY PITCHING THEIR VOICES *INTO A CLAY WATER JAR*

**THE STREET OF 31 OF AUGUST** IN SAN SEBASTIAN, SPAIN, COMMEMORATES THE DATE IN 1813 WHEN AN ANGLO-PORTUGUESE ARMY, "LIBERATING" THE TOWN FROM A FRENCH OCCUPA-TION ARMY, DESTROYED 564 OF ITS 600 HOUSES, SPARING ONLY THIS *ONE STREET, IN WHICH THE "LIBERATORS" HAD THEIR HEADQUARTERS*

147

BAUCHI TRIBESMEN OF NIGERIA RIDE THEIR HORSES WEARING ONLY LEATHER AND IRON SPURS

## THE KING WHO DIDN'T MEASURE UP TO HIS CROWN

KING JAMES II OF ENGLAND AT HIS CORONATION ON APRIL 23, 1685, FOUND HIS CROWN WAS SO MUCH TOO LARGE THAT IT SLIPPED DOWN OVER HIS FACE— IT WAS CONSIDERED A SINISTER OMEN -- AND 3 YEARS LATER THE MONARCH WAS FORCED TO FLEE HIS KINGDOM AND LATER DIED IN EXILE

THE TORBAY BONNET A SHELLFISH HAS A SHELL THAT LOOKS EXACTLY LIKE THE LIBERTY CAP OF THE FRENCH REVOLUTION

THE COVERS OF EVERY BOOK OWNED BY QUEEN MARGARET of Navarre (1552-1615) - BECAUSE MARGARITA MEANS PEARL IN LATIN - WERE STUDDED WITH LARGE ORIENTAL PEARLS

PUSHMATAHA (1765-1834) a Choctaw Indian chief, BECAUSE HIS FOLLOWERS NEVER FOUGHT U.S. SOLDIERS BECAME THE ONLY FULL-BLOODED INDIAN TO BE GIVEN THE FUNERAL OF A U.S. MAJOR GENERAL

THE **MOSQUE** of DAI ANGA in Lahore, Pakistan, BUILT BY ZEB-UN-NISA, WHO HAD BEEN NURSE TO MOGUL EMPEROR SHAH JAHAN IN HIS INFANCY, *WAS CONSTRUCTED WITH FUNDS GIVEN BY THE GRATEFUL EMPEROR TO HIS OLD NURSE*

THE **MUDFISH** WHEN THE POOL OF WATER IN WHICH IT LIVES DRIES UP, CAN SURVIVE UNTIL THE POOL REFILLS *BY HIBERNATING IN THE MUDDY BOTTOM FOR AN ENTIRE SEASON*

THE **BERTELSMANN PUBLISHING HOUSE** IN GÜTERSLOH, GERMANY, *WAS CONSTRUCTED IN 1868 ON STILTS ABOVE A FIRE DEPARTMENT STABLE*

SIR **JOHN LADE** (1759-1838) AN ENGLISH SPORTSMAN IN 1781 BECAME THE FIRST MAN TO *WEAR LONG TROUSERS IN PUBLIC*

A **HOUSE** IN GEISLINGEN, GERMANY, USES AS ITS REAR WALL *THE ANCIENT TOWN WALL*

T<sup>HE</sup> **FIRST** SEE-THROUGH FASHIONS

DANCERS IN THE NEW HEBRIDES, IN THE SOUTH SEAS, WEAR WEB COSTUMES *WOVEN BY SPIDERS ON SPECIAL CONICAL FORMS*

T<sup>HE</sup> **"ALLAH IS GREAT" ARCH** of Isfahan, Iran, IS SO NAMED BECAUSE ARAB TRAVELERS BEHOLDING THE BEAUTY OF ISFAHAN THROUGH THE ARCH, INVARIABLY EXCLAIMED: *"ALLAH IS GREAT"*

T<sup>HE</sup> **NEST** OF THE **MUD DAUBER** *RESEMBLES A MUSICAL INSTRUMENT KNOWN AS THE PIPES OF PAN*

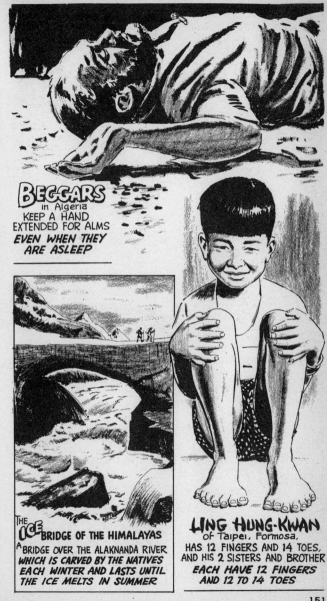

**BEGGARS** in Algeria KEEP A HAND EXTENDED FOR ALMS *EVEN WHEN THEY ARE ASLEEP*

THE **ICE** BRIDGE OF THE HIMALAYAS A BRIDGE OVER THE ALAKNANDA RIVER *WHICH IS CARVED BY THE NATIVES EACH WINTER AND LASTS UNTIL THE ICE MELTS IN SUMMER*

**LING HUNG-KWAN** of Taipei, Formosa, HAS 12 FINGERS AND 14 TOES, AND HIS 2 SISTERS AND BROTHER *EACH HAVE 12 FINGERS AND 12 TO 14 TOES*

## THE SUGAR-COATED TEMPLE
Partabgarh, India

A SPRING INSIDE THE BUILDING PRODUCES SUGAR WHEN ITS WATER IS DISTILLED — *AND THE TEMPLE WALLS ARE SATURATED WITH MOLASSES*

## SHIH CH'UNG T'ANG

A MINISTER OF EMPEROR TAO KUNG of China

WAS EXECUTED IN 1813 FOR TREASON

*BUT SHIH WAS LATER PROVED INNOCENT SO THE EMPEROR BELATEDLY ORDERED THE DEATH SENTENCE ANNULLED*

TO FURTHER ATONE FOR HIS MISTAKE THE EMPEROR ERECTED 100,000 STATUES OF BUDDHA

**EVERY VISITOR** to the "city" of Montpellier-le-Vieux, France, MUST PASS BENEATH THIS GIGANTIC STONE DOG a natural stone formation

A **STATUE** OF KING AMBIOTRIX, A RULER SLAIN DEFENDING HIS PEOPLE AGAINST JULIUS CAESAR, IS VISITED BY EVERY WEDDING PARTY IN TONGRES, BELGIUM —*IN THE BELIEF THE BRIDE'S OFFSPRING WILL THUS BE ASSURED COURAGE EQUAL TO THAT OF THE ANCIENT MONARCH*

**THOMAS JEFFERSON** INTRODUCED SPAGHETTI TO AMERICA

THE **ANGLER FISH** OFTEN SWALLOWS A MYCTOPHID FISH *3 TIMES ITS OWN SIZE*

**MINIATURE HOUSES** ON LAKE INLE, IN BURMA, CONSTRUCTED TO SHELTER THE EVIL SPIRITS, ARE VISITED DAILY BY THE BURMESE *WITH FOOD AND DRINKS*

**JULIUS VOSS** *(1768-1832)*
GERMAN PLAYWRIGHT AND NOVELIST
IN A PERIOD OF 40 YEARS WROTE
*90 SUCCESSFUL PLAYS AND 110 NOVELS*

A **TREE** IN CONAKRY, GUINEA, WHICH GREW OUT OF THE *EMPTY BARK OF A DEAD TREE*

BRENNAN
| MICHAEL | DORINDA | ELLEN | ROBERT | DORINDA |
|---------|---------|-------|--------|---------|
| AGE 38 | 32 | 7 | 5 | 2 |

DIED FEB. 21, 1858

**TOMBSTONE** IN GRASS VALLEY, CALIFORNIA, OF THE FAMILY OF MICHAEL BRENNAN *WHO KILLED HIMSELF, HIS WIFE AND 3 CHILDREN BECAUSE HIS GOLD MINE DID NOT PAN OUT* SOMEONE ELSE DUG DOWN LOWER IN THE SAME SPOT AND FOUND THE NORTH STAR MINE -- WHICH MADE HIM FABULOUSLY WEALTHY

THE **DEVIL FISH** of Africa IS SO TERRIFYING IN APPEARANCE THAT PARENTS USE IT AS THE "BOGY" *TO FRIGHTEN DISOBEDIENT CHILDREN*

THE **KATYDID** HAS ITS EARS IN ITS FRONT LEGS

154

**MEN** OF THE SEPIK REGION OF NEW GUINEA WEAR A CONICAL HEADDRESS TRIMMED WITH SHELL MONEY, SHARKS' TEETH AND FLYING-FOX FUR, THAT IS NEVER REMOVED *-- EVEN IN DEATH*

**THE MONK WHO WRESTLED A PANTHER FOR 45 MINUTES!**
FATHER FRANÇOIS de THANDLA, FRENCH CAPUCINE MONK, ATTACKED ON A HUNTING TRIP IN RAMBHAPUR, INDIA, BY A PANTHER THAT HAD BEEN HIT BY 2 ARROWS, *GRAPPLED WITH THE ANIMAL WITH HIS BARE HANDS FOR 45 MINUTES - SUFFERING 35 WOUNDS --* *A COMPANION FINALLY KILLED THE PANTHER WITH A BULLET*

**WALLAGIE** A MALAY WOODCUTTER OF CAPE TOWN, SO. AFRICA, TO WIN A BET OF $5 *ATE 14 WATERMELONS*

**THE MURRE** AN ARCTIC BIRD *IS DOOMED IF IT LANDS ON THE ICE* IT IS UNABLE TO TAKE OFF AGAIN AND IS KILLED BY CROWS

**ONE WING** of the Abbey of Bouldonne, France, HAS BEEN RECONSTRUCTED AS A LUXURIOUS RESIDENCE ALTHOUGH ALL THE REST OF THE STRUCTURE HAS BEEN *A DESOLATE RUIN SINCE THE FRENCH REVOLUTION*

## THE LIGER

IN THE BLOEMFONTEIN ZOO, SOUTH AFRICA, IS A CROSS BETWEEN *A LION AND A TIGER*

**LICHEN BUGS** ARE SO CALLED BECAUSE THEY *RESEMBLE THAT GRAY FUNGUS*

## THE MATHEMATICIAN WHO DIED BECAUSE HE FAILED A SIMPLE PROBLEM

THE MARQUIS de CONDORCET (1743-1794) A CELEBRATED PHILOSOPHER AND MATHEMATICIAN, HAVING ORDERED AN OMELET AT AN INN IN CLAMART WHILE A FUGITIVE FROM A DEATH SENTENCE IMPOSED BY THE FRENCH REVOLUTIONARIES, WAS ASKED BY THE TAVERN KEEPER HOW MANY EGGS HE WANTED IN IT --WHEN THE MARQUIS ANSWERED, "A DOZEN," THE INNKEEPER SUMMONED THE AUTHORITIES BECAUSE HE KNEW *ONLY AN ARISTOCRAT WOULD BE SO IGNORANT OF THE NUMBER OF EGGS REQUIRED FOR AN OMELET*

THE **LIFE OF RILEY**
MICHAEL LYNN RILEY, Jr. LIVES ON *RILEY* STREET, IN OGDEN, IN *RILEY* COUNTY, KANSAS

THE **GREAT NAVIGATION STONES** ON THE ISLAND OF ARORAE, IN THE GILBERT GROUP, ACTUALLY WERE USED BY NATIVES, TOGETHER WITH THE STARS, *TO DETERMINE NAVIGATION DIRECTIONS BY TRIANGULATION*

**ORHIPPUS** OF MEGARA A GREEK RUNNER WHO WON THE 209-YARD DASH IN THE OLYMPIC GAMES OF 720 B.C., WAS THE LAST GREEK ATHLETE FOR 1,114 YEARS *TO COMPETE IN CLOTHING* BUT HE LOST HIS SHORTS IN THE MIDDLE OF THE RACE

**THE CASTLE OF RECHBERG** IN GERMANY, HAS BEEN OWNED BY THE SAME FAMILY *CONTINUOUSLY FOR 791 YEARS*

**A GRAVESTONE RIDDLE** in Bristol, England— IN THOSE TIMES SINGLE WOMEN WERE ADDRESSED AS "MISTRESS" — WHICH WAS CONTRACTED TO "MRS."

IN MEMORY of Mr. THOMAS RIDLEY And Mrs. SARAH RIDLEY Being Brother and Sister yet Never Married Erected Anno Dom. 1739

**BUSHMEN** of South Africa TO STALK OSTRICHES *DON THE STUFFED HEAD, NECK, BODY AND WINGS OF AN OSTRICH*

**THE PROPHECY THAT WAS STRANGELY FULFILLED BY A DAGGER** KING PHILIP II of Macedonia, WARNED BY AN ORACLE TO "BEWARE OF A CHARIOT" NEVER RODE IN ONE DURING HIS LIFETIME, BUT DURING HIS DAUGHTER'S WEDDING CEREMONY HE WAS SLAIN BY AN ASSASSIN'S DAGGER—*THE HILT OF WHICH WAS ORNAMENTED WITH A CARVING OF A CHARIOT* ( 336 B.C. )

## PHILIP *THE* MAGNANIMOUS
[ 1504-1567 ]
WHO RULED HESSEN FOR 58 YEARS, WENT HUNTING FROM DAWN UNTIL 9 A.M. AND AGAIN FROM 3 P.M. TO 9 P.M. *EVERY DAY FOR 49 YEARS*

**ALLAN BALDWIN**
of Staten Island, N.Y.,

A 15-YEAR-OLD HIGH SCHOOL STUDENT, MADE A HOLE IN ONE *THE 4th TIME HE EVER PLAYED GOLF*

**FUNERAL PROCESSIONS**
OF HIGH DIGNITARIES IN BURMA ALWAYS FEATURE ROLLING PYRAMIDS ON WHICH ARE HUNG HUNDREDS OF *TEAPOTS AND SPITTOONS-- WHICH ARE PRESENTED TO THE MONKS PARTICIPATING IN THE CEREMONY*

**BLACK PORCELAIN TEETH**
WERE WORN BY MEMBERS OF THE ROYAL COURT OF THAILAND UNTIL 1935 ON ALL *CEREMONIOUS OCCASIONS*

160

**ANNIBALE CARRACCI**
(1560-1609)
WAS A TAILOR'S APPRENTICE UNTIL HIS SKETCHES OF 2 THUGS WHO HAD HELD HIM UP RESULTED IN THEIR ARREST *--AND REVEALED HE WAS ONE OF THE FINEST ARTISTS OF HIS TIME* IN RECOGNITION OF HIS ARTISTIC ABILITY HE IS BURIED BESIDE RAPHAEL

*"Bobbie"* A COLLIE OWNED BY G. FRANK BRAZIER, OF SILVERTON, ORE., LOST IN INDIANA ON A CROSS-COUNTRY AUTOMOBILE TRIP, FOLLOWED THE FAMILY CAR A TOTAL OF 3,000 MILES *--WAS SIGHTED BY FRIENDS OF THE BRAZIERS ON ITS JOURNEY-- AND FINALLY FOLLOWED THEM HOME AFTER 6 MONTHS ON THE TRAIL*

**STREETCARS**
IN MANCHESTER, ENGLAND, IN THE EARLY 1900'S *DELIVERED PARCEL POST PACKAGES*

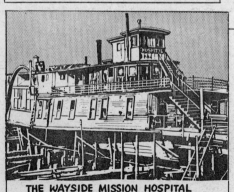

**THE WAYSIDE MISSION HOSPITAL**
at Seattle, Wash., *ONCE SERVED AS A COASTAL STEAMER*

*"MIDGEY"* A CAT 24 YEARS OLD

THE INSCRIPTION OVER THE ANCIENT ACADEMY OF ATHENS, GREECE

ΜΗΔΕΙΣ ΑΓΕΩΜΕΤΡΟΣ ΕΙΣΙΤΩ

"LET NO UNGEOMETRIC PERSON ENTER" IS REPEATED OVER THE ENTRANCE TO RHODES HOUSE, IN OXFORD, ENGLAND, BUT BY CHANGING ONE WORD IT READS:

ΜΗΔΕΙΣ ΚΑΠΝΟΦΟΡΟΣ ΕΙΣΙΤΩ

"LET NO SMOKING PERSON ENTER"

**SCHOOLCHILDREN** IN SWAT, PAKISTAN, CARRY THEIR BOOKS WRAPPED IN A HANDKERCHIEF ON THEIR HEAD IN THE BELIEF *IT WILL MAKE THEM SMARTER*

**MEDICINE MEN** OF THE MAMBUNDU TRIBE, AFRICA, BELIEVE THEY CAN DISPEL ANY ILLNESS *SOLELY BY DANCING*

NONE OF US EVER VOTED FOR ROOSEVELT OR TRUMAN

EPITAPH OF ROBERT R. HALLENBECK IN THE CEMETERY AT ELGIN, MINN.

THE **CITY CHURCH** of Freudenstadt, Germany, HAS A SEPARATE WING FOR ITS FEMALE PARISHIONERS *SO THE 2 SEXES CANNOT SEE EACH OTHER DURING SERVICES*

## THE BUTCHER'S BROOM
IS A PLANT *WITHOUT LEAVES*—
WHAT APPEAR TO BE LEAVES
ARE ACTUALLY BRANCHES BENEATH
WHICH ITS FRUIT GROWS

## THE TUNYAS
MEMBERS OF AN AFRICAN TRIBE
FISH IN LAKE LEOPOLD WHILE
BALANCING THEMSELVES ON
*3 TREE TRUNKS LASHED TOGETHER
TO FORM A CRUDE RAFT*

## KING CHILPERIC I
WHO RULED THE FRANKS
FROM 561 TO 584
MADE MARITAL INFIDELITY
PUNISHABLE BY DEATH
—THEN HAD HIS OWN WIFE
STRANGLED IN 568 SO
HE COULD MARRY ONE OF
HIS SERVING WOMEN

**CLONMACNOISE** a town in Ireland,
IN A PERIOD OF *759 YEARS*
WAS INVADED BY ENEMY
WARRIORS *47 TIMES*—

*THE TOWN CEASED TO
EXIST IN 1552 - BUT
ONLY AFTER THE DANES
HAD BURNED IT TO THE
GROUND 10 TIMES*

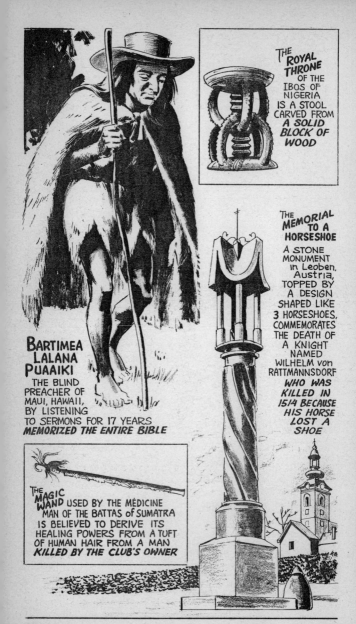

**THE ROYAL THRONE** OF THE IBOS OF NIGERIA IS A STOOL CARVED FROM *A SOLID BLOCK OF WOOD*

**BARTIMEA LALANA PUAAIKI** THE BLIND PREACHER OF MAUI, HAWAII, BY LISTENING TO SERMONS FOR 17 YEARS *MEMORIZED THE ENTIRE BIBLE*

THE **MEMORIAL TO A HORSESHOE** A STONE MONUMENT IN Leoben, Austria, TOPPED BY A DESIGN SHAPED LIKE 3 HORSESHOES, COMMEMORATES THE DEATH OF A KNIGHT NAMED WILHELM von RATTMANNSDORF *WHO WAS KILLED IN 1514 BECAUSE HIS HORSE LOST A SHOE*

THE **MAGIC WAND** USED BY THE MEDICINE MAN OF THE BATTAS of SUMATRA IS BELIEVED TO DERIVE ITS HEALING POWERS FROM A TUFT OF HUMAN HAIR FROM A MAN *KILLED BY THE CLUB'S OWNER*

**THE JUSTICE STONE OF BANGANGTE,** Kamerun, Africa
AN OATH, SWORN ON THIS SACRED STONE *IS ACCEPTED AS THE TRUTH DESPITE ANY JUDICIAL EVIDENCE TO THE CONTRARY*

**DANIEL KNIGHT** (1695-1756) of Luton, England, MADE HIS COFFIN IN THE SHAPE OF A CUPBOARD AND USED IT IN HIS HOME FOR **30 YEARS** *HE CHANGED HIS DATE OF DEATH EACH YEAR – BUT NONE OF THE 30 DATES HE CARVED IN THE COFFIN WAS THE CORRECT ONE, JUNE 11, 1756*

**EUGENE MUGEL BEY** (1808-1890) A FRENCH ENGINEER *SAVED THE EGYPTIAN PYRAMIDS FROM DESTRUCTION* VICEROY ABBAS I, of Egypt, HAD ORDERED USE OF THE PYRAMIDS' STONES FOR CONSTRUCTION OF A DAM, BUT MUGEL PERSUADED HIM TO RESCIND HIS DECISION

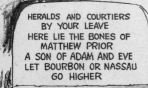

HERALDS AND COURTIERS BY YOUR LEAVE HERE LIE THE BONES OF MATTHEW PRIOR A SON OF ADAM AND EVE LET BOURBON OR NASSAU GO HIGHER

**EPITAPH** OF ENGLISH POET MATTHEW PRIOR, A COMMONER, IN WESTMINSTER ABBEY

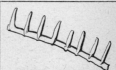

**MONEY** IN New Guinea ONCE WAS IN THE FORM OF DOGS' TEETH, FASTENED TO A SHORT STICK

**THE STAR SNAIL**
TOWS ITS EGGS IN A SPAWNING RIBBON THAT *WEIGHS 3 TIMES AS MUCH AS THE SNAIL*

**BOARS' TUSKS**
THAT HAD GROWN INTO A DOUBLE CIRCLE WERE SO RARE IN THE NEW HEBRIDES, THAT A NATIVE DESIRING TO SEE ONE HAD TO PAY AN ADMISSION FEE OF *ONE LIVE PIG*

**THE COMPLETE ILIAD AND ODYSSEY**
COMPRISING 48 BOOKS, ONCE WERE TRANSCRIBED IN LETTERS OF GOLD *ON THE 100-FOOT-LONG INTESTINE OF A SNAKE—* THIS MOST ASTOUNDING WORK OF LITERATURE WAS DESTROYED WHEN FIRE RAZED THE GREAT LIBRARY OF BYZANTIUM IN 476

**ROADSIDE SHRINES** in the Tyrol mountains HAVE WOODEN DOORS WHICH ARE NAILED SHUT EACH WINTER *TO PROTECT THEM FROM THE DEEP SNOWS WHICH ALWAYS BURY THEM*

**THE MAN WHOSE TEETH WERE EACH WORTH 2 HORSES**

EDWARD WOODVILLE AN ENGLISH SOLDIER WHO LOST 6 FRONT TEETH FIGHTING FOR QUEEN ISABELLA OF SPAIN AGAINST THE MOORS --AS REIMBURSEMENT FOR HIS LOSS WAS *AWARDED 12 THOROUGHBRED HORSES*
(1486)

**MANY-POINTED ARROWS** USED BY THE MARIA GONDS OF India **TO HUNT BIRDS AND HUMANS**

**PREHISTORIC HORSES**
MILLIONS OF YEARS AGO *WERE ONLY AS TALL AS A RABBIT SITTING ON ITS HAUNCHES*

A **SMALL AIRPLANE** PURCHASED BY CARL CROW, OF MUSKOGEE, OKLA., SECONDHAND, FROM A MAN IN PERRY, OKLA., HAD THE IDENTIFICATION NUMBER 23898 -- *THE SAME NUMBER AS CROW'S HOME PHONE*

THE **FRESHWATER DRUMFISH** FEEDS ON MOLLUSKS AND MUSSELS, GRINDING UP THE HARD SHELLS *WITH TEETH LOCATED IN ITS THROAT*

THE **ORIGIN OF THE MAXIS**
TROUSERS WORN IN JAPAN EARLY IN THE 19th CENTURY *WERE MORE THAN TWICE AS LONG AS THE LEGS OF THEIR WEARER*

167

**DR. THEODORE KOESTER**
PIONEER SETTLER OF
NEW BRAUNFELS, TEXAS,
*WAS THE TOWN'S APOTHECARY,
PHYSICIAN--AND BAKER*

THE
*SLEEPING
KNIGHT*
NEAR
ESCH ON
THE SAUER,
LUXEMBOURG,
*NATURAL
ROCK
FORMATION*

**A HOUSE OF WORSHIP**
IN NEW YORK CITY
IS SHARED BY THE VILLAGE
PRESBYTERIAN CHURCH AND
THE BROTHERHOOD SYNAGOGUE,
AND A JOINT BOARD HAS
ADMINISTERED ITS AFFAIRS
WITHOUT A SINGLE NOTE OF
DISCORD *IN 15 YEARS*

**JAMES M. ASHLEY** (1822-1896)
TERRITORIAL GOVERNOR OF MONTANA,
HAVING ONCE BEEN ROBBED IN A
HOTEL ROOM, ALWAYS PLACED
HIS MONEY IN ONE OF HIS SOCKS
--*AND THREW IT ACROSS THE ROOM*
HE INSISTED SINCE HE HAD
TROUBLE FINDING THE SOCK
AGAIN IN DAYLIGHT, NO
BURGLAR WOULD LOCATE
IT IN THE DARK

THE **CALENDAR** USED BY VEY TRIBESMEN OF W. AFRICA CONSISTS OF 2 CORDS--ONE WITH *7 WOODEN MARKERS* FOR THE DAYS OF THE WEEK AND THE OTHER WITH *4 MARKERS* FOR THE WEEKS IN EACH MONTH

**A BLUE CRANE**
CAUGHT IN EDEN, N.Y., IN 1931, HAD IN ITS CROP-- *140 TROUT*

**THE BIG BRAIN**
**IVAN TURGENEV** (1818-1883) THE RUSSIAN AUTHOR, HAD A BRAIN WHICH PROVED AFTER HIS DEATH TO WEIGH *4½ POUNDS*

THE **ROCK TABLE** of **MT. REDJAF** Africa
A STONE SLAB, 45 FEET WIDE AND 46 FEET LONG, DEPOSITED BY A GLACIER ON A STONE SUPPORT 11 FEET HIGH

**CAKES** BAKED IN CRAILSHEIM, GERMANY, STILL ARE UNIQUELY SHAPED TO DERIDE A BESIEGING ENEMY THAT WAS DRIVEN OFF BY THE TOWN'S DEFENDERS *590 YEARS AGO*

## JOHANNES von BENDER
(1713-1798) AN AUSTRIAN FIELD MARSHAL *SERVED IN THE ARMY FOR 65 YEARS --TAKING PART IN 29 CAMPAIGNS, 12 BATTLES AND 9 SIEGES*

**ELZIE TREMAIN**

A BARBER IN EVERETT, WASH., HAS CUT THE HAIR OF **6** **GENERATIONS** OF THE SAME FAMILY

THE HERB OF THE EVIL WOMAN IS THE NAME OF A MEXICAN PLANT *WHICH STINGS UNWARY PASSERSBY WHEN IT IS DISTURBED*

### FATHER PETER DE SMET

(1801-1872) A BELGIAN MISSIONARY TO THE AMERICAN INDIANS, CHALLENGED BY A CROW CHIEF TO PROVE THAT HE WAS PROTECTED BY THE GREAT SPIRIT, *WALKED UP TO A WILD BUFFALO AND PATTED THE BULL ON ITS HEAD*

### A SWISS POSTAGE STAMP

PRINTED IN GERMAN, FRENCH AND ITALIAN --WITH THE NAME OF THE COUNTRY IN LATIN

### THE FLOATING RAINMAKER

A STATUE OF SHIN U RAGO, A MONK REVERED AS A RAINMAKER, HAS DRIFTED ALONG THE SHORES OF BURMA FOR **40** YEARS *AND COASTAL COMMUNITIES BELIEVE THEY CAN ASSURE RAIN MERELY BY GIVING IT SHELTER IN THEIR HARBOR*

JOHN BLAIR
DIED OF SMALLPOX
COWBOY THROWED
ROPE OVER FEET
AND DRAGGED HIM
TO HIS GRAVE

**EPITAPH** IN BOOTHILL CEMETERY,
TOMBSTONE, ARIZONA

THE **TOWER** OF THE CATHEDRAL OF
LAUSANNE, SWITZERLAND,
**HOUSES THE LAST NIGHT
WATCH IN EUROPE**
THROUGHOUT THE NIGHT A GUARD
CALLS OUT THE TIME EACH HOUR
AND WATCHES FOR FIRES

THE **TURBANS**
WORN BY THE PIRATES OF ZANZIBAR
WERE SO LONG THAT THEY COULD BE
USED TO TRUSS UP A PRISONER,
*MAKING HIM LOOK LIKE AN EGYPTIAN MUMMY*

A **ROMAN DEFENSE**
AGAINST ENEMY
CAVALRY
CONSISTED OF
BALLS OF IRON
*-BRISTLING WITH
LONG, SHARP
POINTS*

## THE TWINS

THE "CASTALIA"
LAUNCHED IN 1874 FOR
SERVICE IN THE
ENGLISH CHANNEL,
TO ACHIEVE GREATER
STABILITY IN THE
ROUGH WATERS
*WAS BUILT WITH
2 HULLS* -
IT SERVED FOR
9 YEARS, BUT WAS
SCRAPPED BECAUSE
IT PROVED TOO SLOW
AND CUMBERSOME

THE MALE
LUMPFISH
GUARDS THE
EGGS LAID BY
THE FEMALE
*--FASTING
THE ENTIRE
50 DAYS
UNTIL THEY
HATCH*

## THE PIG LADY

A WOMAN IN LONDON, ENGLAND,
WHO HAD A PERFECTLY PROPORTIONED
BODY AND WAS AN EXPERT PIANIST
*HAD THE HEAD AND FACE OF A PIG-*
SHE ALWAYS DINED FROM A SILVER TROUGH

173

THE **GREAT STAIRWAY** of **CALTAGIRONE** ITALY 26 FEET WIDE AND 426 FEET LONG HAS 142 STEPS -- OF WHICH *100 FORM THE THRESHOLDS OF OCCUPIED DWELLINGS*

**THE WORLD'S MOST HOSPITABLE HOSTS**
THE CAVE DWELLERS of LLUCH, on the Island of Majorca, FOR CENTURIES HAVE OFFERED SHELTER AND FOOD TO ANY TRAVELER FOR 72 HOURS -- *FREE!*

*FRANCESCO* **AVELLONI** (1756-1837) of NAPLES, ITALY, WHO WROTE 600 PLAYS OF 5 ACTS EACH, WAS INSPIRED TO BECOME A PLAYWRIGHT *BY A COLORFUL THEATRICAL POSTER*

### THE STRANGEST COURTSHIP IN ALL HISTORY

KING ASAN II, WHO RULED BULGARIA FROM 1223 TO 1241, WOOED AND WON AS HIS BRIDE, IRENE, DAUGHTER OF PRINCE THEODORE of EPIRUS, *AFTER HAVING DEFEATED HER FATHER IN BATTLE, TAKEN HIM PRISONER--AND BLINDED HIM*

### SALT LAKE

ON CARMEN ISLAND, MEXICO, PRODUCES PURE TABLE SALT SO RAPIDLY THAT WHEN ALL OF ITS SALT CONTENT IS REMOVED *IT REPLENISHES IT AGAIN IN JUST 7 DAYS*

### SIR JOHN SUCKLING

(1609-1642) THE ENGLISH POET, COULD SPEAK LATIN FLUENTLY *AT THE AGE OF 5*

### ORCHARD ORIOLES

BUILD TWIN NESTS— ONE FOR THE FEMALE AND HER EGGS AND THE OTHER FOR THE MALE

THE **S.S. CONSUL**
ENGLAND'S OLDEST PADDLE STEAMER, BUILT IN 1896 IN WEYMOUTH, HAS A SPECIALLY REINFORCED HULL SO THAT IT CAN *BE DELIBERATELY RUN AGROUND ON BEACHES NOT EQUIPPED WITH PIERS*

## CAPTAIN LOUIS d'ASSAS (1733-1760)

A FRENCH OFFICER CAPTURED AT KLOSTERKAMP, GERMANY, SACRIFICED HIS LIFE TO WARN HIS COMRADES, AN ACT OF HEROISM THAT WON HIS DESCENDANTS A PENSION FROM THE FRENCH CROWN -- *PAYABLE ANNUALLY AS LONG AS A SINGLE MALE MEMBER OF THE FAMILY SURVIVED*

THE **BIRD**
NATURAL ROCK FORMATION AT LAKE MYVATN, ICELAND -*OVERLOOKING A BIRD SANCTUARY*

JOSEPH BOECK (1804-1900) of Guntramsdorf, Austria, SERVED AS PASTOR OF ITS PARISH FOR **72** YEARS

THE **STANDLEY** CHASM IN THE MacDonnell Mountains of Australia, **20** FEET WIDE AND **500** FEET DEEP, IS A CLEFT SO DARK THAT A MAN STANDING AT THE BOTTOM OF IT *CAN SEE STARS IN THE DAYTIME*

A **HUMAN IMAGE** IS DISPLAYED OVER THE ENTRANCE TO THE RAJAH'S PALACE, in Timor, Indonesia -- A MEMORIAL TO AN OLD CUSTOM OF ACTUALLY *IMPALING THE BODY OF A CRIMINAL THERE*

THE **BELFRY** OF THE CHURCH OF BESSE, FRANCE, *WAS ORIGINALLY THE GATE OF THE TOWN WALL*

THE **LARVA** OF A NICARAGUAN INSECT CALLED THE PHANTOM IS INDISTINGUISH- ABLE FROM THE MOSS IN WHICH IT HIDES

THE **WEDDING CEREMONY** of the Bhils of India IS LITERALLY A **TYING OF THE KNOT** THE GROOM'S CLOAK IS KNOTTED TO THE BRIDE'S VEIL--AND BOTH WEAR MASKS SO THE HUSBAND WILL BE THE FIRST TO BEHOLD THE COUNTENANCE OF HIS BELOVED AS A MARRIED WOMAN

THE **RESTAURANT** IN THE SWISS MUSEUM OF TRANSPORT, IN LUCERNE, SWITZERLAND, IS THE 90-TON STEAMER, "RIGI", WHICH WAS OPERATED ON LAKE LUCERNE FOR **105** YEARS

A **TRANSPARENT GELATIN TRAP** IS BUILT BY OIKOPLEURA, A SEA CREATURE, TO CATCH MINUTE PLANKTON WHICH ARE WASHED IN THROUGH SMALL OPENINGS AT EACH END OF **THE UNDERSEA "GLASS HOUSE"**

**FLOCKS OF SPARROWS** OFTEN TIGHTLY FOLD THEIR WINGS AND **FLY THROUGH THE HOLES IN A MESH FENCE**

**THE FLOATING GARDENS of BURMA**
THE LAKE OF SMILES HAS FLOATING ACRES OF DIRT IN WHICH GROW BOTH *VEGETABLES AND FLOWERS*

**THE PASTOR WHO WAS GRANTED HIS MOST ARDENT WISH**
THE REV. ARMSTRONG CORNSILK (1844-1925) AN INDIAN, OF CHEROKEE COUNTY, N.C., WHO PRAYED DAILY THAT HE MIGHT DIE WHILE WORKING FOR THE LORD, *FELL DEAD ON A SUNDAY MORNING IN HIS PULPIT AT THE INSTANT HE COMPLETED HIS BIBLE READING* ( Aug. 22, 1925 )

**SMALL MASKS of the GOD BACCHUS**
WERE HUNG IN THE VINE-YARDS IN ANCIENT ROME IN THE BELIEF THAT EVERY AREA THE IMAGE FACED AS IT WAS TWIRLED ABOUT BY THE WIND WOULD *YIELD GREATER CROPS*

**GEORGE JACOBS** OF CAMDEN COUNTY, N.C., ENLISTED IN THE ARMY OF THE CONFEDERACY *WHEN HE WAS ONLY 9 YEARS AND 9 MONTHS OF AGE*

179

## THE FIRST SOAP

MADE FROM ANIMAL SUET AND BEECHWOOD ASHES WAS USED BY ROMAN MATRONS *TO BLEACH THEIR HAIR*— ONLY LATER DID THEY LEARN ITS VALUE AS A CLEANSER

### THE SLEEPER
ISLAND OF CHAUSEY IN THE ENGLISH CHANNEL— *NATURAL ROCK FORMATION*

A HIGHBALL

### A TENNIS BALL
BATTED OVER A ROOF BY AN 8-YEAR-OLD BOY LANDED IN THE MIDDLE OF A WEDDING RECEPTION *-PLOPPING INTO A GLASS OF CHAMPAGNE WITHOUT BREAKING THE GLASS*

### THE EMPEROR
WHO PREFERRED TO BE A DOORMAN

**ISAAC COMNENES,** WHO RULED THE EASTERN HALF OF THE ROMAN EMPIRE FROM 1057 TO 1059, ABDICATED HIS THRONE TO SPEND THE REMAINDER OF HIS LIFE *AS A DOORMAN OF THE MONASTERY OF STUDE*

### THE PUNISHMENT
OF A CONVICTED THIEF ON THE ISLAND OF SOKOTRA, IN THE INDIAN OCEAN, IS AMPUTATION OF HIS RIGHT HAND *-- AND SEVERED HANDS CAN BE SEEN HANGING FROM TREES ALONG THE BUSIEST HIGHWAYS*

**AKELA TRIBESMEN** OF THE CONGO HAVE THE INCISOR TEETH KNOCKED OUT OF BOTH JAWS, AND THEREAFTER MUST CUT THEIR FOOD BY SAWING IT *AGAINST A KNIFE HELD BETWEEN THEIR TOES*

THE **ABBEY of FIESOLE** Italy WAS BUILT IN 1462 BEHIND THE FAÇADE OF ANOTHER STRUCTURE -THAT HAD BEEN BUILT *434 YEARS EARLIER*

**THE GREAT WESTERN** FIRST CAR FERRY OF THE GREAT WESTERN RAILWAY WAS BUILT ON THE CLYDE RIVER, IN GLASGOW, SCOTLAND, IN 1866, THEN DISMANTLED AND SHIPPED ACROSS THE ATLANTIC IN *10,878 PIECES*

## CHIEF HENDRICK
(1680-1755)
OF THE MOHAWK INDIANS, KEPT A RECORD OF THE NUMBER OF MEN HE KILLED BY CUTTING AN X FOR EACH ONE ON A TREE --*A TOTAL OF 39 X's*

A *CUP* FOUND IN A CAVE AT LEITMERITZ, CZECHOSLOVAKIA, HAS AS A DESIGN A CAVEMAN'S CALENDAR *PAINTED ON IT 4,000 YEARS AGO*

The **PLAGUE STONE** Bodenbach, Germany, IT WAS ERECTED BY HANS PITZEN IN FULFILLMENT OF A VOW THAT HE WOULD CONSTRUCT A CROSS ON THAT SPOT IF A PLAGUE ENDED AND HE NO LONGER HAD TO **HAUL CORPSES FROM THE STRICKEN VILLAGE—** THE CORPSES HE WAS CARRYING WHEN HE MADE THE VOW *WERE THE LAST ONES*

**MONUMENT ROCK**
OFF THE ISLAND OF CLARION, MEXICO, A NATURAL FORMATION 200 FEET HIGH, *HAS ARCHES, PINNACLES, TURRETS AND A CUPOLA*

## SIR EDWARD LAKE

( 1600-1674 ) WOUNDED **16** TIMES IN THE BATTLE OF EDGEHILL, IN ENGLAND'S CIVIL WAR, AND DEPRIVED OF THE USE OF HIS LEFT HAND BY A BULLET, CONTINUED TO WIELD HIS SWORD WITH HIS RIGHT HAND, *GUIDING HIS HORSE BY HOLDING ITS BRIDLE IN HIS TEETH*— HE RECOVERED AND LIVED ANOTHER 32 YEARS

A **2-PIECE WOOL DRESS** FOUND IN A GRAVE NEAR BORUM ESHÖI, DENMARK, IS PERFECTLY PRESERVED ALTHOUGH IT WAS WORN *3,500 YEARS AGO*

THE **NO. 1 WIFE** OF THE CHIEF OF THE DAN TRIBE, IN LIBERIA, TO SYMBOLIZE THE FACT THAT SHE NEVER HAS TO WORK OR HURRY, WEARS THROUGH-OUT HER LIFETIME *METAL ANKLETS THAT WEIGH* **26 POUNDS**

THE **UNDERWEAR** WORN BY JAPANESE SAMURAI OF THE 19th CENTURY BENEATH THEIR ARMOR WAS *MADE OF IRON*

A **CHURCH** IN WACO, TEXAS, THAT WAS BUILT IN A *SINGLE DAY* January 11, 1911

THE **MALARMAT**, A FISH, RUNS ALONG THE BOTTOM OF THE MEDITERRANEAN ON *TINY FEET WHICH ARE EXTENSIONS OF ITS FINS*

**THE FIDDLER'S STONE** AT THE ENTRANCE TO CASTLE CALDWELL, NEAR LOUGH ERNE, IRELAND, IS A MEMORIAL TO DENIS McCABE, A FIDDLER WHO DROWNED -- *AND A WARNING TO OTHER FIDDLERS AGAINST OVERIMBIBING WHISKEY*

**ITALIAN COMMANDOS** IN WORLD WAR I WERE TESTED FOR COURAGE BY REQUIRING THEM TO STAND AT ATTENTION WHILE A HEAVY ROCK WAS SWUNG OVER THEM SO CLOSELY *THAT IT BRUSHED OFF THEIR CAPS*

**DAILY DIARY ENTRIES**
MUST BE MADE BY THE HEAD
OF EACH FAMILY OF THE
MOSSO TRIBE, of Yunnan, China,
RECORDING EVERYTHING
OF INTEREST IN
*PICTURE WRITING*

"MOUNT'N MUSIC"
DRUMMERS in Kaduna, Nigeria,
PLAY IN PARADES WHILE MOUNTED
*ON THE SHOULDERS OF FRIENDS*

**LOTHROP COOKE**
WAS A FEARED AND RESPECTED
SHERIFF IN NIAGARA COUNTY, N.Y.
*ALTHOUGH HE HAD ONLY
ONE LEG AND WALKED
WITH A CRUTCH* 1821

**FAREWELL** IS AN INTERJECTION, A NOUN, A VERB, AN ADJECTIVE, AND AN ADVERB

**JOHN TAYLOR** (1711-1775) OF BIRMINGHAM, ENGLAND, MADE A FORTUNE DECORATING THE LIDS OF SNUFF BOXES BY A SECRET PROCESS --WHICH AFTER HIS DEATH WAS REVEALED AS SIMPLY PRESSING *INTO THE DAMP ENAMEL HIS THUMBPRINT*

from an old print

**THE VELOCIPEDRAISIAVAPORIANA** INVENTED IN FRANCE IN 1818, USED STEAM FOR POWER--BUT 2 FIREMEN HAD TO WALK *BEHIND IT TO STOKE THE FURNACE*

THE **HORSES** OF SULTAN ALI, OF THE NORTHERN CAMEROONS, IN PARADES ALWAYS WEAR **SILK TROUSERS**

**RICHARD W. JONES** (1837-1911) SOUTHERN EDUCATOR, SERVED AS PRESIDENT *OF 4 COLLEGES*

186

### KING SARGON II

PAGAN RULER OF ASSYRIA, WORE LARGE EARRINGS IN THE SHAPE OF A CROSS **722 YEARS BEFORE THE BIRTH OF CHRIST**

### THE SUNFISH
DIGS A NEST FOR THE FEMALE IN THE SANDY RIVER BOTTOM *–THEN SWIMS GUARD OVERHEAD*

### THE THIEF WHO BECAME A KING!

**YACOUB ibn LEITS** of Bost, in Seistan, Asia, BROKE INTO THE HOME OF SALIH ben NASR BUT CONFESSED HIS CRIME THE NEXT DAY—AN ACT WHICH SO IMPRESSED HIS POLITICALLY POWERFUL VICTIM THAT SALIH MADE IT POSSIBLE FOR YACOUB TO BECOME *RULER OF KHORASAN AND SEISTAN ONLY 10 YEARS LATER!*

THE FORMER BURGLAR FOUNDED A DYNASTY THAT RULED THE **2** COUNTRIES FOR 126 YEARS TILL 1005

### LAKE KURNAS
ON THE ISLAND OF CRETE, GREECE, OVERFLOWS WITH PERFECT REGULARITY EVERY **5** YEARS– ITS WATERS RISE 15 FEET AND POUR INTO THE MEDITERRANEAN

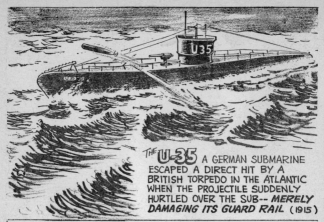

THE *U-35* A GERMAN SUBMARINE ESCAPED A DIRECT HIT BY A BRITISH TORPEDO IN THE ATLANTIC WHEN THE PROJECTILE SUDDENLY HURTLED OVER THE SUB-- *MERELY DAMAGING ITS GUARD RAIL* (1915)

CAN YOU DRAW THE 5 ENTWINED CIRCLES OF THE OFFICIAL OLYMPIC FLAG IN ONE CONTINUOUS LINE -*WITHOUT CROSSING A LINE*?

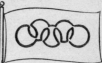

HOW TO DRAW THE 5 ENTWINED CIRCLES OF THE OFFICIAL OLYMPIC FLAG IN ONE CONTINUOUS LINE --*WITHOUT CROSSING A LINE*

## THE CASTLE THAT WAS GIVEN AS A TIP!
LE COUDRAY- MONTPENSIER, Seuilly, France, WAS PRESENTED BY KING FRANÇOIS I TO HIS VALET *FOR HELPING THE MONARCH REMOVE HIS CLOAK!* KING FRANÇOIS HAD NO GOLDPIECE IN HIS POCKET --*SO HE THREW HIS SERVANT THE DEED TO THE CASTLE* [1520]

**HENRY STUART** (1725-) (1807)

PRETENDER TO THE BRITISH THRONE WHO CALLED HIMSELF KING HENRY IX, WAS A BITTER ENEMY OF KING GEORGE III, YET WHEN HENRY FLED FROM THE FRENCH REVOLUTION, PENNILESS, *KING GEORGE GRANTED HIM AN ANNUAL PENSION OF $20,000*

**THE SKULL** OF THE MARQUIS OF MONTROSE IS THE COAT OF ARMS OF THE HAMOND FAMILY BECAUSE IN 1650 A HAMOND ANCESTOR DARED REMOVE THE HEAD OF THE MARQUIS FROM *THE SPIKE ON WHICH IT WAS EXHIBITED IN EDINBURGH AFTER HIS EXECUTION*

**THE JERRYMUNGLUM** WHICH PREYS ON TERMITES *HAS 2 NOSES* -- ONE AT THE TIP OF EACH OF ITS LEG-LIKE FEELERS

**THE CAMEL** NEAR CASTELMEUR, BRITTANY, NATURAL ROCK FORMATION

**SAMUEL BIRCH** (1757-1841) WAS LORD MAYOR OF LONDON, A LIEUTENANT COLONEL IN THE MILITIA, A SUCCESSFUL PLAYWRIGHT, AN OUTSTANDING POET, AND A PROFESSIONAL PASTRY CHEF --*SIMULTANEOUSLY*

THE **MEMORIAL** in Custer, So. Dakota, TO HORACE N. ROSS, WHO DISCOVERED GOLD IN THE BLACK HILLS, IS A CONCRETE OBELISK IN WHICH HAVE BEEN IMBEDDED **314** DIFFERENT KINDS OF MINERALS, ROCKS, FOSSIL BONES AND PETRIFIED WOOD

## The **OLD SOLDIER**

**SERGEANT ANDREW WALLACE**
(1730-1835) a native of Scotland

AT THE AGE OF **46** ENLISTED IN THE AMERICAN ARMY DURING THE REVOLUTION AFTER HAVING ALREADY FOUGHT IN **2** WARS — AND CONTINUED AS AN AMERICAN SOLDIER *UNTIL HE WAS 81 YEARS OF AGE* WALLACE LIVED TO THE AGE OF 105

**"CAESAR"**
A BULLDOG *WAS THE FIRST POLICE DOG* IT WAS TRAINED IN 1897 BY FRIEDRICH LAUFER, THE POLICE COMMISSIONER OF SCHWELM, GERMANY

**BOMBARDMENT BEANS**
WHICH GROW ON A SO. AFRICAN CREEPER, WHEN DISTURBED BY AN UNWARY PASSERBY FIRE A BURST OF TINY THORNS WHICH WORK THEIR WAY THROUGH ANY CLOTHING AND *BLISTER THE SKIN*

190

**HOMES** NEAR THE LOGONE RIVER, IN NIGERIA, AFRICA, ARE BUILT OUT OF THE STRAW OF CEREAL PLANTS, AND WHEN THE RISING RIVER THREATENS TO INUNDATE THE VILLAGE *THE HOUSES ARE ROLLED UP AND CARRIED TO HIGHER GROUND*

THE **MARQUIS** de **CONTADES** (1704-1793) MARSHAL OF FRANCE, WAS SO SHOCKED WHEN A REVOLUTIONARY TRIBUNAL COMPRISING HIS OWN SERVANTS SENTENCED HIM TO DEATH AS A ROYALIST *THAT HE DROPPED DEAD AT THEIR FEET*

**EVERY YOUNGSTER** TAKING PART IN AN ANNUAL PROCESSION in Barcelona, Spain, *MUST HAVE A SNUBNOSE* THEY PARADE IN MILITARY FORMATION, BUT INSTEAD OF ARMS THEY CARRY ON THEIR SHOULDERS OVERSIZE *KNIVES, FORKS and SPOONS*

A **TALL** POLE IS ERECTED OVER THE GRAVE OF A CHIEFTAIN IN TIMOR, IN THE MALAY ARCHIPELAGO, *TO DISPLAY THE JAWBONES AND HORNS OF ALL THE CATTLE EATEN AT THE SUMPTUOUS FUNERAL FEAST*

JOHN MOTTEUX (1766-1843) OF BEACHAMWELL, ENGLAND, NEVER ONCE TOOK MEDICINE *IN 77 YEARS*

THE STONE "TREE TRUNKS" *TREES* IN GUELL PARK, IN BARCELONA, SPAIN, **GROW FROM STONE COLUMNS THAT LOOK LIKE TREE TRUNKS**

THE **CATERPILLAR** RANCH HOUSE (Homaledra Heptathalama) A CATERPILLAR OF THE SOUTHERN U.S. CONSTRUCTS A HOUSE CONSISTING OF 7 OR 8 ROOMS -- *ALL ON ONE LEVEL -- THE UNDER- SIDE OF A LEAF*

THE **YELLOW WARBLER** OUTWITS THE COWBIRD WHEN IT LAYS EGGS IN THE WARBLER'S NEST BY BUILDING A SECOND OR EVEN A THIRD STORY ON ITS NEST -- EFFECTIVELY *SEALING OFF THE TRESPASSER'S EGGS*

MR. PRESIDENT, YOU'RE WANTED ON THE PHONE!

**NO PRESIDENT OF THE U.S.** HAD A TELEPHONE IN HIS OFFICE **UNTIL 1929** FROM 1878 UNTIL 1929 THE PRESIDENT'S TELEPHONE WAS IN A BOOTH IN AN OUTER HALLWAY